T0283490

Like-Minded Allies?

Indo-Pacific Partners' Views on Possible Changes in
the U.S. Relationship with Taiwan

JEFFREY W. HORNUNG, MIRANDA PRIEBE, BRYAN ROONEY,
PATRICK HULME, NOBUHIKO TAMAKI, YU INAGAKI

Sponsored by the Sasakawa Peace Foundation

RAND NATIONAL SECURITY RESEARCH DIVISION

For more information on this publication, visit **www.rand.org/t/RRA739-7**.

About RAND

The RAND Corporation is a research organization that develops solutions to public policy challenges to help make communities throughout the world safer and more secure, healthier and more prosperous. RAND is nonprofit, nonpartisan, and committed to the public interest. To learn more about RAND, visit www.rand.org.

Research Integrity

Our mission to help improve policy and decisionmaking through research and analysis is enabled through our core values of quality and objectivity and our unwavering commitment to the highest level of integrity and ethical behavior. To help ensure our research and analysis are rigorous, objective, and nonpartisan, we subject our research publications to a robust and exacting quality-assurance process; avoid both the appearance and reality of financial and other conflicts of interest through staff training, project screening, and a policy of mandatory disclosure; and pursue transparency in our research engagements through our commitment to the open publication of our research findings and recommendations, disclosure of the source of funding of published research, and policies to ensure intellectual independence. For more information, visit www.rand.org/about/principles.

RAND's publications do not necessarily reflect the opinions of its research clients and sponsors.

Published by the RAND Corporation, Santa Monica, Calif.
© 2023 RAND Corporation
RAND® is a registered trademark.

Library of Congress Cataloging-in-Publication Data is available for this publication.

ISBN: 978-1-9774-1149-5

Cover: Getty images.

About This Report

Policy experts in the United States are in the midst of a debate about the future of the U.S. relationship with Taiwan. Some commentators have called for the United States to strengthen ties with the island, including by explicitly committing to Taiwan's defense. Other analysts argue that the United States should maintain the policy of strategic ambiguity, where the United States arms Taiwan and maintains the capability to defend it without committing to intervene militarily in the event of war. A third group argues that the United States should gradually wind down security ties with the island. The debate over these options has focused on how a change in U.S. policy toward Taiwan would affect the likelihood of an invasion by China. This report considers an often-overlooked question: How would U.S. regional allies respond to a change in U.S. policy toward Taiwan? This report focuses on the views of Japan, the Republic of Korea, and the Philippines. This research was completed in February 2023.

RAND Center for Analysis of U.S. Grand Strategy

This research was sponsored by the Sasakawa Peace Foundation and conducted within the RAND Center for Analysis of U.S. Grand Strategy. The center's mission is to inform the debate about the U.S. role in the world by more clearly specifying new approaches to U.S. grand strategy, evaluating the logic of different approaches, and identifying the trade-offs each option creates. Initial funding for the center was provided by a seed grant from the Stand Together Trust. Ongoing funding comes from RAND supporters and from foundations and philanthropists.

The center is an initiative of the International Security and Defense Policy Center of the RAND National Security Research Division (NSRD). NSRD conducts research and analysis for the Office of the Secretary of Defense, the U.S. Intelligence Community, the U.S. State Department, allied foreign governments, and foundations.

For more information on the RAND Center for Analysis of U.S. Grand Strategy, see www.rand.org/nsrd/isdp/grand-strategy or contact the center director (contact information is provided on the webpage).

Acknowledgments

We thank Aya Murata of the Sasakawa Peace Foundation for her support and active engagement throughout this project. We also appreciate comments from reviewers Naoko Aoki (RAND) and Bonny Lin (Center for Strategic and International Studies).

Summary

Issue

U.S. foreign policy experts have been debating options for future U.S. policy toward Taiwan, including

1. making an explicit commitment to defend the island in the event of war, a policy known as *strategic clarity*
2. maintaining the long-standing U.S. policy of *strategic ambiguity,* or not explicitly stating whether the United States would defend Taiwan in the event of war
3. gradually decreasing U.S. support to Taiwan and encouraging the island to become more self-sufficient.

Discussions of these options tend to focus on how each would affect China's calculus on invading the island. However, a change in U.S. policy toward Taiwan could have many other effects. This report focuses on one of the other dimensions with potentially significant implications for U.S. interests: how U.S. allies respond to changes in Washington's relationship with Taipei. In particular, we consider the possible responses of three U.S. allies: Japan, the Republic of Korea (ROK), and the Philippines. With an understanding of allies' potential responses, U.S. leaders can assess the trade-offs associated with options for future policy toward Taiwan and craft options to mitigate costs and risks.

Approach

We reviewed the history of U.S. allies' relationships with Taiwan and the contemporary relations each ally has with the United States, China, and Taiwan. We also interviewed policymakers and experts in Japan, the ROK, and the Philippines about their views on hypothetical policy changes the United States could undertake to signal either a firmer or looser relationship with Taiwan. We discussed potential changes in U.S. diplomatic, intelligence, military, and economic relations with Taiwan. We took steps to encourage candid responses and mitigate the risk of strategic answers (i.e., answers intended to influence U.S. policy rather than describing genuine beliefs), such as keeping interviewees anonymous. This analysis offers a snapshot of how allies might respond in peacetime to a change in U.S. foreign policy in the current strategic setting. Future research should consider how allies' responses might differ as dynamics in the region change or in the event of a crisis or conflict.

Key Findings

We have the following findings about allies' responses to changes in U.S. policy toward Taiwan in a near-term peacetime context.

Allies' Potential Reactions to Increased U.S. Support to Taiwan

Japan favors increases in many forms of U.S. diplomatic and military support to Taiwan and would adopt similar policies up to a point. Japan sees intrinsic value in preventing the People's Republic of China (PRC) from controlling Taiwan and fears that the possibility of a Chinese invasion of the island is growing. Therefore, Japan supports policies it believes will increase the U.S. ability to deter China from attacking Taiwan, such as more high-level U.S. visits to and statements in support of Taiwan, as well as increases in U.S. arms sales to and military presence near the island. Although Japan is not likely to recognize Taiwan as an independent nation or commit to defend the island, it would likely follow the U.S. lead by adopting similar policies if the United States were to increase other forms of diplomatic support to Taiwan.

The Philippines and the ROK do not support increasing many forms of U.S. diplomatic and military support to Taiwan and would likely not adopt such policies themselves. The Philippines and South Korea are more concerned with stability in the Taiwan Strait than Taiwan's status. Both countries worry that increasing U.S. support to Taiwan could undermine stability by provoking China to increase military activities around the island. The two countries therefore oppose highly publicized U.S. diplomatic support to Taiwan, which they believe increases tensions with China without strengthening the U.S. ability to deter China, but are open to more subtle measures. Officials in South Korea supported increased arms sales to Taiwan and U.S. regional military presence but raised concerns about U.S. military activities in or near Taiwan. Officials in the Philippines also generally opposed an increased military presence on or around Taiwan, but recent actions suggest that they too support an increased U.S. regional presence.

The three countries are neutral about increased U.S. intelligence sharing and are supportive of increases in U.S. economic relations with Taiwan. Intelligence issues were seen as primarily bilateral between the United States and Taiwan. The three believe that Taiwan's economic integration in the region benefits all parties and does not provoke China.

Allies' Potential Reactions to Reductions in U.S. Support to Taiwan

These allies oppose reductions in U.S. support to Taiwan, which they believe might lead to instability in the Taiwan Strait. All three countries worry that any reduction in U.S. support to Taiwan could make China more likely to attack Taiwan.

Japan, the ROK, and the Philippines would see a reduction in U.S. support to Taiwan as a signal of waning U.S. commitment to their own security. This is notable because Japan, the ROK, and the Philippines have mutual defense treaties with the United States, which include an explicit U.S. promise to support these countries if attacked, something Taiwan no longer enjoys.

The value that Japan and the ROK place on their alliances with the United States suggests that concerns about U.S. reliability would lead them to first try to draw the U.S. closer. Interviewees' comments on potential responses to reductions in U.S. support to Taiwan over their objections were limited. Nevertheless, our interviews offer some insights into allies' views of their options. Interviews reinforced government statements about Japan's deep security concerns regarding China and determination to push back against China's growing influence in the region. Moreover, interviewees emphasized Japan's view that its alliance with the United States is fundamental to Japan's security. This suggests that Japan's initial response to concerns about U.S. reliability would likely be to try to pull the United States closer. There was no indication that Japan would consider building closer ties with China in response.

Similarly, official statements and interviews show that the ROK sees the U.S. alliance as an indispensable part of countering the Democratic People's Republic of Korea (DPRK), the ROK's greatest threat. The ROK does not believe that China's influence on the DPRK alone can provide the ROK with security. Therefore, in the face of concerns about U.S. reliability, the ROK too would likely try first to pull the United States closer.

Past behavior suggests that the Philippines' response to concerns about U.S. reliability would depend on who is in power and on China's recent behavior. Interviewees had divergent views about how they would respond to a U.S. decision to reduce support to Taiwan. Currently, the Philippines sees China as a significant threat. However, past Philippine leaders have sometimes attempted closer relations with China in periods when China's behavior was less assertive. Therefore, we assess that the Philippines' responses to concerns about U.S. reliability may depend more on the context, specifically who is leading the Philippines and China's recent behavior.

Implications

The findings of this report have implications for U.S. policymakers considering whether and how to change U.S. policy toward Taiwan. U.S. treaty allies see a direct stake in U.S. actions vis-à-vis Taiwan. U.S. policymakers should therefore expect these countries to react to any U.S. policy changes toward Taiwan and consider how those reactions affect U.S. regional interests. Allies' reactions should be part of the broader assessment of the trade-offs associated with changes in U.S. policy toward Taiwan. While the debate in the United States about U.S. policy toward Taiwan has been overtaken by a narrow discussion over the value of retaining strategic ambiguity versus a shift to strategic clarity, there is a much broader—and richer—discussion to be had over the policy options the United States has for signaling closer or weaker ties with Taiwan, how allies would respond to each option, and whether allies would follow suit by adopting similar policies.

Contents

Figure and Tables

Figure

Tables

CHAPTER 1

Introduction

The United States has long held a policy of *strategic ambiguity* regarding its role in the defense of Taiwan. The United States provides Taiwan with arms and maintains a capability to defend Taiwan, but it does not commit to defending the island. For example, the Taiwan Relations Act (TRA), a key part of U.S. policy toward Taiwan, states that any effort to determine the future of Taiwan by other than peaceful means would be of "grave concern" to the United States, suggesting that a military response is possible.[1] However, the TRA does not commit the United States to intervene militarily in the event of an attack on the island.

Given growing Chinese power and military activities near Taiwan, U.S. policy analysts and academics have been debating whether to continue the policy of strategic ambiguity. Some commentators argue that *strategic clarity*, which would involve an unambiguous public commitment to Taiwan's defense, would more effectively deter China from attacking the island. U.S. President Joseph Biden appears sympathetic to this logic, as he has repeatedly indicated that the United States would defend Taiwan if it were attacked, although officials in his administration insist that the U.S. policy of strategic ambiguity has not changed.[2] But a policy of strategic clarity remains con-

---

[1] Public Law 96-8, Taiwan Relations Act, 1979.

[2] "Biden Tells 60 Minutes U.S. Troops Would Defend Taiwan, but White House Says This Is Not Official U.S. Policy," CBS News, September 18, 2022; The White House, "Remarks by President Biden in a CNN Town Hall with Anderson Cooper," October 21, 2021; "Full Transcript of ABC News' George Stephanopoulos' Interview with President Joe Biden," ABC News, August 19, 2021. For an example of other officials reiterating that U.S. policy has not changed, see U.S. Department of State, "Remarks: Secretary Antony J. Blinken and Philippine Secretary of Foreign Affairs Enrique Manalo at a Virtual Press Availability," August 6, 2022.

troversial. Some analysts worry that statements like Biden's provoke China and embolden Taiwan to take steps toward independence. In this view, the United States would be better off maintaining strategic ambiguity.[3] Other analysts go further, arguing that the United States should gradually reduce security relations with Taiwan while encouraging the island to be responsible for its own defense.[4]

As intense as these arguments have become, analysts on all sides often ignore concrete policy actions that could help illuminate *specific* policy choices the U.S. administration could take to achieve a desired end. More critically, these debates tend to focus on the likely Chinese response to a change in U.S. policy. Seldom—if ever—do these debates consider how other regional actors, particularly U.S. allies, would interpret such changes in U.S. policy. Given the important role these allies play in current U.S. regional strategy—and potentially in a regional military contingency—this report focuses on their views.[5]

Specifically, we ask how three U.S. treaty allies in the Indo-Pacific (Japan, the Republic of Korea [ROK], and the Philippines) might respond to a change in U.S. policy vis-à-vis Taiwan. We focus on these three allies because they are most proximate to Taiwan and therefore most likely to be affected by a conflict over the island and called upon to support U.S. forces in the event the United States intervenes to defend Taiwan. We consider how these three countries would respond to peacetime U.S. policy changes intended to signal either stronger U.S. support to or, conversely, a weaker relationship with Taiwan. While the current discourse tends to focus narrowly on U.S. declaratory policy about its defense commitment to Taiwan, this report considers the full range of tools the United States has at its disposal to adjust its relationship with Taiwan, including policies in the diplomatic, information, military, and economic domains. In so doing, we

---

[3] Stephen Wertheim, "On Taiwan, President Biden Should Listen to Senator Biden," Carnegie Endowment for International Peace, September 20, 2022.

[4] See, for example, Barry R. Posen, *Restraint: A New Foundation for U.S. Grand Strategy*, Cornell University Press, 2014, p. 104; Ted Galen Carpenter and Eric Gomez, "East Asia and a Strategy of Restraint," *War on the Rocks*, August 10, 2016.

[5] The White House, *National Security Strategy*, October 1, 2022; U.S. Department of Defense, *National Defense Strategy of the United States of America*, 2022.

seek to shed light on how changes in U.S. policies in each domain would be interpreted by three of the most geographically proximate U.S. treaty allies. Future research should also consider how other allies, such as Australia or even members of the North Atlantic Treaty Organization, might respond to changes in U.S. policy toward Taiwan.

The Contemporary U.S. Debate

In the United States, most of the public debate regarding Taiwan currently revolves around the question of declaratory policy. That is, should the United States clearly state its intention to defend Taiwan, a policy referred to as *strategic clarity*, or maintain its traditional policy of not specifying its intent, a policy referred to as *strategic ambiguity*. While the policy of strategic clarity seeks to deter China from attacking Taiwan by clarifying U.S. intentions, the U.S. policy of strategic ambiguity has sought to balance two competing goals: deterring China from invading Taiwan and dissuading Taiwan from taking steps (i.e., declaring independence) that could provoke a Chinese invasion. Holding out the possibility of U.S. intervention is intended to deter China while at the same time creating some doubt in Taiwan about U.S. support to deter the island's leaders from adopting risky policies that court conflict.

Advocates of strategic clarity want the United States to intervene to defend Taiwan if China attacks. This group believes that the United States can best deter China by making its intentions clear. According to this logic, strategic ambiguity could lead China to underestimate U.S. willingness to defend Taiwan. The possibility of Chinese misperception is more consequential than in the past, given large increases in Chinese military power. Strategic clarity aims to reduce the risk that China will launch a war with the mistaken belief that the United States will not intervene (or will only provide limited support to Taiwan).[6] Advocates of strategic clarity do not

---

[6] Richard Haass and David Sacks, "American Support for Taiwan Must Be Unambiguous: To Keep the Peace, Make Clear to China That Force Won't Stand," *Foreign Affairs*, September 2, 2020; Gary J. Schmitt and Michael Mazza, "The End of 'Strategic Ambiguity' Regarding Taiwan," *The Dispatch*, September 17, 2020. See also Charles L. Glaser, "A U.S.-China Grand Bargain? The Hard Choice Between Military Competition and

believe that an explicit U.S. security guarantee would embolden Taiwan to adopt policies that make conflict more likely. This group argues that Taiwan recognizes that actions such as declaring independence would be counter to its interests.[7] Some who favor strategic clarity note that this risk could be further reduced by making a commitment that, while explicit, is conditional on Taiwan's behavior. That is, the United States could state that in the event Taiwan declared independence, the United States would not come to its defense.[8] On the whole, then, those in favor of strategic clarity believe that the benefits of reducing China's misperceptions outweigh this risk. Given their view of costs and benefits of strategic clarity, the policy's proponents argue the United States should make its commitment to Taipei unambiguous.[9]

Proponents of maintaining strategic ambiguity argue that a change in declaratory policy is not necessary and could, in fact, be dangerous. According to this logic, an explicit security guarantee could cause the very war that supporters of strategic clarity seek to deter in one of two ways: by provoking China to attack to forestall growing U.S. support to Taiwan or emboldening pro-independence groups in Taiwan to take steps that provoke a Chinese invasion.[10] Among those who favor maintaining strategic ambiguity, there are both those who seek to maintain U.S. policy as is and those who believe that the United States should increase its support for Taiwan within the bounds of strategic ambiguity.[11]

Accommodation," *International Security*, Vol. 39, No. 4, 2015. For a general discussion of misperception and conflict, see James D. Fearon, "Rationalist Explanations for War," *International Organization*, Vol. 49, No. 3, 1995; Alex Weisiger, *Logics of War: Explanations for Limited and Unlimited Conflicts*, Cornell University Press, 2013.

[7] Haass and Sacks, 2020; Raymond Kuo, "'Strategic Ambiguity' Has the U.S. and Taiwan Trapped," *Foreign Policy*, January 18, 2023.

[8] Kuo, 2023; "Should the United States Pledge to Defend Taiwan? Foreign Affairs Asks the Experts," *Foreign Affairs*, November 15, 2022.

[9] Haass and Sacks, 2020.

[10] Bonnie S. Glaser, "A Guarantee Isn't Worth the Risk," *Foreign Affairs*, September 24, 2020.

[11] See, for example, discussions in Evan A. Feigenbaum and Barbara Weisel, "Deepening the U.S.-Taiwan Economic Partnership," Carnegie Endowment for International

There is also a third group that argues that the United States should not defend Taiwan. According to this line of thinking, China's growing power, strong national interests in Taiwan, and nuclear weapons mean that a war over Taiwan could be very costly and risky. These analysts argue that there are not sufficient U.S. interests at stake in the island's status to risk a great-power war that could escalate to nuclear use. Some in this camp support maintaining strategic ambiguity in the short term while helping Taiwan increase its ability to defend itself. Beyond that, these analysts have not discussed specific ways they would like the U.S. relationship with Taiwan to change. In broad terms, however, these analysts seek to gradually downgrade U.S. security relations with Taiwan while helping Taiwan become more self-sufficient.[12]

What is missing from these debates is (1) a discussion of policy options the United States has at its disposal to signal its intention to strengthen or downgrade its relations with Taiwan and (2) how U.S. treaty allies in the region might respond to changes in U.S. Taiwan policy. In the next section, we outline what these policy options are. In the chapters that follow, we consider how Japan, the ROK, and the Philippines might respond to a change in U.S. policies toward Taiwan.

Policy Options for Signaling a Change in the U.S. Relationship with Taiwan

The debate about U.S. policy toward Taiwan has focused on one mechanism the United States has for signaling its commitment to Taiwan: a change in declaratory policy. Underlying this narrower debate about declaratory

Peace, March 4, 2021; Paul Haenle and Evan Medeiros, "Why the U.S. Needs to Say Less and Do More on Taiwan," Carnegie Endowment for International Peace, July 18, 2022.

[12] Carpenter and Gomez, 2016; Jasen J. Castillo, "Passing the Torch: Criteria for Implementing a Grand Strategy of Offshore Balancing," in Richard Fontaine and Loren DeJonge Schulman, eds., *New Voices in Grand Strategy*, Center for a New American Security, 2019, p. 31; Lyle J. Goldstein, "How Progressives and Restrainers Can Unite on Taiwan and Reduce the Potential for Conflict with China," *Responsible Statecraft*, April 17, 2020; Patrick Porter, "The United States Should Not Defend Taiwan," *National Review*, December 20, 2021; Posen, 2014, p. 104.

policy is a broader debate about whether the United States should increase, maintain, or decrease its level of support for Taiwan. Once the United States makes that decision, it has multiple tools to try to signal any changes. This report looks beyond this narrow debate over declaratory policy to understand allied perspective on a wider range of tools the United States has at its disposal. We group U.S. policy tools into four broad categories.

Diplomatic. The United States could signal a change in its U.S. relationship with Taiwan by changing the number or rank of government officials visiting Taiwan, the frequency and choice of language in statements that warn China against invading or coercing Taiwan, and the number and type of references to Taiwan in joint statements with allies and partners. The United States could also change its level of support for Taiwan's participation in international meetings and organizations under its own name that do not require statehood for membership, such as the World Health Organization, the Asia Pacific Economic Cooperation grouping, or even the International Olympic Committee. Another option, and one often discussed in the current debate, is either declaring unambiguously that the U.S. would defend Taiwan, increasing the ambiguity in statements on the U.S. role in Taiwan's defense, or declaring that the United States would not fight to defend Taiwan.

Military. The United States could signal a greater commitment to Taiwan through an increase in peacetime military activities near Taiwan (e.g., naval presence in the Taiwan Strait) or joint exercises with Taiwan's military. The United States currently has a small number of military personnel in Taiwan engaged in training activities. Some proponents of increased U.S. support to Taiwan have proposed a larger presence to signal a firmer commitment.[13] The United States could increase the quantity or quality of arms it sells to Taiwan to signal greater support. Although less specific, the United States could also increase the number and capability of forces in the region with an eye on using this more robust presence for deterrence purposes in peacetime and operational purposes in a Taiwan contingency. Conversely, the United States could signal a weaker commitment to Taiwan by decreasing

---

[13] Henry Olsen, "Biden Is Right on Taiwan. Now He Needs a Staff That Won't Undercut Him," *Washington Post*, September 19, 2022.

the number of military activities and U.S. military presence, as well as limiting arms sales.

Economic. Should the United States seek to signal a stronger commitment to Taiwan, it could pursue more economic agreements with Taiwan or help the economy better integrate into regional economic relationships and institutions. One example is the Comprehensive and Progressive Agreement for Trans-Pacific Partnership. Conversely, should the United States seek to signal a weaker commitment to Taiwan, it could limit its bilateral economic interactions with Taiwan or withdraw support from Taiwan integrating into regional economic relationships.

Information. The amount and type of intelligence sharing between Taipei and Washington could also be a signal of U.S. intent toward the island. It may seem counterintuitive to think of intelligence sharing as a signal, since it is often done out of the public eye. However, presumably the United States would let other allies in the region know about any changes in intelligence-sharing arrangements, and Chinese intelligence would detect some indications of any change.

Methodology

This report asks how the hypothetical U.S. policy changes discussed in the previous section might affect allied perceptions and behavior. To answer this question, we began by reviewing the history of bilateral relations Taiwan has with Japan, the ROK, and the Philippines. We then considered each country's relations with China, the United States, and Taiwan. Finally, we examined how each country may potentially respond to changes in U.S. policy on Taiwan. Our sources of information included strategic documents and statements from allied governments, commentary from experts in each allied country, and interviews with government officials and experts.

Government documents we reviewed generally did not discuss U.S. or allied relations with Taiwan in great depth, likely due to the sensitivity of the topic and the lack of formal diplomatic ties. Expert commentary did not generally discuss allied views of U.S. relations with Taiwan in detail either. For this topic, therefore, interviews became a key source for understanding allies' perspectives about future U.S. policy options. We traveled to the Philippines, South Korea, and Japan in the fall of 2022 to interview analysts who are knowledgeable about their country's relations with China, Taiwan, and the United States as well as officials (both current and former) in the countries' executive and legislative branches and government research organizations. We conducted ten discrete interviews in Japan, ten in the ROK, and seven in the Philippines. Twelve of these interviews were conducted with current policymakers; of the remainder, the majority were conducted with former or retired policymakers and bureaucrats. Most frequently, we conducted these interviews with a single participant. In a few cases, an interviewee invited a colleague to join our discussion, so we conducted a smaller number of interviews with two participants. One session in the Philippines included several interviewees in a group setting. In theory, group interviews could lead participants to withhold true preferences on a controversial topic. However, in practice, interviewees in these settings often disagreed with one another, suggesting they felt comfortable sharing their views among close colleagues.

Because relations with Taiwan remain a sensitive topic with these countries as they navigate their relations with China, the United States, and Taiwan, we were alert to the possibility that some policymakers and analysts might be reluctant to meet with us or to speak candidly on the topic. To encourage interviewees to speak freely, we conducted interviews anonymously. Because government employees might be most reluctant to speak on these topics, we supplemented official meetings with discussions with former officials and outside analysts.[14]

Every country has debates about its foreign policies, and there are, of course, a range of views on national security within each government and among policy commentators. For example, in all the countries we examined, there are business leaders and some experts who believe that the government should do more to encourage closer relations with China. While these are important issues to understand, they are beyond the scope of our

---

[14] Jeffrey M. Berry, "Validity and Reliability Issues in Elite Interviewing," *PS: Political Science & Politics*, Vol. 35, No. 4, 2002; Delphine Alles, Auriane Guilbaud, and Delphine Lagrange, "Interviews in International Relations," in Guillaume Devin, ed., *Resources and Applied Methods in International Relations*, Springer, 2018; Layna Mosley, "Introduction: 'Just Talk to people'? Interviews in Contemporary Political Science," in Layna Mosely, ed., *Interview Research in Political Science*, 2013.

study. Rather, we focused on the dominant views within each country that shape official policy, which we obtained through policymakers' speeches and interviews, government documents, and interviews. Therefore, in the chapters that follow, when we refer to a country's perspective, we are describing the viewpoints we heard in interviews, as well as those revealed in official government policy. Future research could benefit from considering the full range of views present within each country in greater detail to better gauge the forces that may pull policies in different directions.

There are two additional caveats that we recognized and want to make explicit. First, our research, conducted in the fall of 2022, represents a snapshot in time. Political dynamics in each of the country case studies do not stop after our research is complete. For example, when we spoke to individuals in Manila and Seoul, the Ferdinand Marcos Jr. and Yoon Suk-yeol administrations were still relatively new. Therefore, their policies relating to the United States, China, and Taiwan were still in their early stages. The individuals we spoke to, as well as the primary data we collected, reflect views at this particular point in time. In the case of the Philippines, there were differences between what we heard in interviews and what was subsequently implemented in administration policies, which we discuss in Chapter 5. Subsequent developments in Japan and South Korea reinforced, rather than ran counter to, what we heard in interviews.

Our analysis does not consider all future strategic changes in the region and world that may cause allies' views to evolve going forward. Our research should therefore be viewed as a first step to understanding the likely reactions from U.S. allies, a topic that has not been fully considered in the current debate.

Second, we recognize that interviewees might respond strategically rather than genuinely to questions about their countries' likely responses to future changes in U.S. policy. For example, some interviewees may want the United States to increase support to Taiwan. Focusing on the costs and risks in their responses could be a means by which they seek to influence U.S. policymakers who might read this report. There is no way to entirely prevent strategic responses. However, we mitigated this potential source of bias by asking the interviewees to assume the United States had already decided to change relations with Taiwan (i.e., upgrading or downgrading U.S. relations with Taiwan). We then asked them to compare the trade-offs associated with different policy options for doing so (e.g., change in U.S. diplomatic versus military policies).[15]

Report Road Map

The remainder of this report is organized as follows. Chapter 2 provides a history of U.S. policy vis-à-vis Taiwan, setting the background for understanding the current debate over strategic clarity or strategic ambiguity. Chapters 3 through 5 examine each U.S. ally's relationship with Taiwan; views of the United States, China, and Taiwan; and predicted responses to hypothetical changes in U.S. policy toward Taiwan. Chapter 6 synthesizes the findings and discusses implications for U.S. policy.

---

[15] Alles, Guilbaud, and Lagrange, 2018; Philip H. J. Davies, "Spies as Informants: Triangulation and the Interpretation of Elite Interview Data in the Study of the Intelligence and Security Services," *Politics*, Vol. 21, No. 1, 2001.

CHAPTER 2

History of the U.S. Security Relationship with Taiwan

The United States has held a wide variety of policies toward Taiwan. This has ranged from the decision not to defend Chinese Nationalist forces on Taiwan in 1949, to a formal commitment to the island's defense in the 1950s and 1960s, to the current policy of strategic ambiguity that involves U.S. support to Taiwan without a formal commitment to defend the island. This chapter briefly summarizes this changing relationship.

1949–1950: Decision Not to Defend Nationalist Forces on Taiwan

In 1949, after a series of Chinese Communist military victories in the Chinese Civil War, the remnants of the Nationalist force evacuated to Taiwan. The United States had previously supported the Nationalists. But its losses led the Harry Truman administration to debate the strategic importance of the island (then called Formosa) and whether to intervene. The administration ultimately decided against a U.S. military intervention or military aid to the Nationalists on Taiwan.[1] In January of 1950, President Truman and Secretary of State Dean Acheson both declared that the United States would not interfere in the Chinese Civil War and disavowed any intent to defend

---

[1]   John G. Reid and John P. Glennon, eds. *Foreign Relations of the United States, 1949, The Far East and Australasia*, Vol. VII, Part 2, Document 387, U.S. Government Printing Office, 1976; John W. Garver, *The Sino-American Alliance: Nationalist China and American Cold War Strategy in Asia*, M.E. Sharpe, 1999, p. 18.

the island.[2] The administration did, however, continue diplomatic and economic support to the Nationalists.[3]

The decision not to defend Taiwan proved controversial domestically.[4] Some Republicans in Congress attacked the administration for the "final betrayal and sellout of an American ally."[5] Some within the executive branch also sought to reverse the decision. For example, General Douglas MacArthur advocated for the island's defense, describing it as a strategically valuable "unsinkable aircraft carrier."[6] From within the State Department, future Secretaries of State Dean Rusk and John Foster Dulles argued that the administration should "neutralize Formosa, not permitting it either to be taken by Communists or to be used as a base of military operations against the mainland."[7]

Japan and the ROK (or South Korea), not yet U.S. treaty allies, were both concerned about this change in U.S. policy toward Taiwan. In early 1949, the United States had announced that it was ending military support for the ROK. This policy had provoked deep security concerns in South Korea. The change in U.S. policy toward the Chinese Nationalists exacerbated these concerns and contributed to the ROK's decision to press for an alliance with the United States. Japan, still under U.S. occupation, also sought U.S. security assurances after it perceived the United States as "writing off Formosa."[8]

---

[2] Nancy Bernkopf Tucker, *Strait Talk: United States–Taiwan Relations and the Crisis with China*, Harvard University Press, 2011, p. 13; Richard C. Bush, *At Cross Purposes: U.S.-Taiwan Relations Since 1942*, Taylor & Francis Group, 2015, p. 85; National Archives, "The President's News Conference," Harry S. Truman Library, January 5, 1950.

[3] Iain D. Henry, *Reliability and Alliance Interdependence: The United States and Its Allies in Asia, 1949–1969*, Cornell University Press, 2022, pp. 17–18; Garver, 1999.

[4] Garver, 1999, pp. 20–21.

[5] As quoted in Henry, 2022, p. 49.

[6] He Di, "'The Last Campaign to Unify China': The CCP'S Unmaterialized Plan to Liberate Taiwan, 1949–1950," *Chinese Historians*, Vol. 5, No. 1, 1992, p. 13.

[7] Neal H. Petersen et al., eds., *Foreign Relations of the United States, 1950, East Asia and the Pacific*, Vol. VI, Document 183, U.S. Government Printing Office, 1976.

[8] Henry, 2022, pp. 47–50; quote on p. 50.

1950–1955: The United States Declares It Will Defend Taiwan

Ultimately, it was North Korea's invasion of South Korea that caused the Truman administration to revise its Taiwan policy. In coordination with the decision to send American forces to defend the ROK, on June 27, 1950, Truman announced the deployment of the U.S. Seventh Fleet to the Taiwan Strait, explaining that "the occupation of Formosa by Communist forces would be a direct threat to the security of the Pacific area and to United States forces performing their lawful and necessary functions in that area."[9] This was the first explicit U.S. commitment to defend Taiwan against a Communist attack from the mainland.

The United States' position on the legal status of the island also changed. Japan annexed Taiwan and the Pescadores Islands from China in 1895 via the Treaty of Shimonoseki. In 1943, the United States joined the Cairo Declaration, which stated that Taiwan "shall be restored to the Republic of China" at the conclusion of the war.[10] In 1950, however, the United States declared that "the determination of the future status of Formosa must await the restoration of the security in the Pacific, a peace settlement with Japan, or consideration by the United Nations."[11] Efforts to have the United Nations settle the issue were unsuccessful, however, and the eventual peace treaty with Japan did not resolve the island's status. In the 1951 Treaty of San Francisco, Japan "renounced all right, title and claim" to the island group, but to whom title was transferred was deliberately omitted.[12]

The Seventh Fleet continued to patrol the Taiwan Strait throughout the Korean War and after the 1953 Korean Armistice. President Dwight Eisenhower's first State of the Union address even suggested the United States would support the Republic of China (ROC, also known as Taiwan) if it

---

[9] John P. Glennon and S. Everett Gleason, eds. *Foreign Relations of the United States, 1950, Korea*, Vol. VII, U.S. Government Printing Office, 1976, Document 119.

[10] Cairo Declaration, U.S. Department of State Bulletin, 1943.

[11] Bush, 2015, p. 89.

[12] Treaty of Peace with Japan, September 8, 1951.

attacked the mainland.[13] However, behind the scenes, administration officials were deeply concerned that the ROC's goal of retaking mainland
China would draw the United States into war. The United States therefore
attempted to restrain the ROC by placing conditions on its military and
economic support.[14]

1955–1979: U.S. Alliance with Taiwan

The ROC had sought a treaty with the United States since the beginning
of the Eisenhower administration, but it did not come about until the First
Taiwan Strait crisis in 1954.[15] The crisis commenced when PRC forces began
shelling the Nationalist-controlled islands off the Chinese mainland (the
"offshore islands") in what appeared to be a first step toward invading Taiwan.[16] The United States sought a defense treaty with Taiwan to deter a Chinese invasion of the island and believed that, with a treaty, the United States
could more effectively restrain the ROC from offensive military operations
against the mainland.[17] The United States and regional allies (Japan, the
ROK, the Philippines, Australia, and New Zealand) agreed that Taiwan and
the Pescadores islands were important to defend.[18] (See map in Figure 2.1.)
The United States had particular concerns about credibility—that is, how
its response in the Taiwan Strait would affect the perceived reliability of
its commitments elsewhere in East Asia. For example, Eisenhower worried

---

[13] John P. Glennon, David W. Mabon, and Harriet D. Schwar, eds. *Foreign Relations of
the United States, 1952–1954, China and Japan*, Vol. XIV, Part 1, U.S. Government Printing Office, 1985, Document 75.

[14] Victor Cha, *Powerplay: The Origins of the American Alliance System in Asia*, Princeton University Press, 2016, pp. 65–93.

[15] Bush, 2015, pp. 96–97; Henry, 2022.

[16] Thomas E. Stolper, "China, Taiwan, and the Offshore Islands Together with an
Implication for Outer Mongolia and Sino-Soviet Relations," *International Journal of
Politics*, Vol. 15, No. 1/2, 1985.

[17] Henry, 2022, p. 76.

[18] Yang Huei Pang, *Strait Rituals: China, Taiwan, and the United States in the Taiwan
Strait Crisis, 1954–1958*, Hong Kong University Press, 2019; Henry, 2022.

FIGURE 2.1

Map of the Taiwan Strait

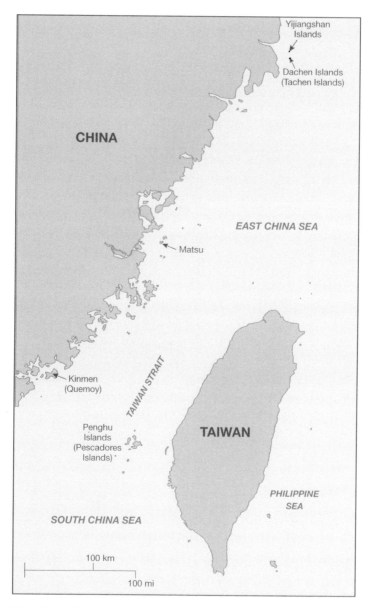

SOURCE: RAND-created map. Names that the United States historically used to refer to offshore islands, in parentheses, come from Jacob Van Staaveren, *Air Operations in the Taiwan Crisis of 1958*, USAF Historical Division Liaison Office, 1962.

that "the psychological effect in the Far East of deserting our friends on Formosa would risk a collapse of Asiatic resistance to the Communists"[19] more broadly. The "offshore islands," still under Nationalist control, however, were another matter. Many U.S. allies and members of Congress felt these islands had limited strategic value and the risks of defending them heavily outweighed any prospective benefit.[20]

To gain Senate ratification of an alliance treaty, the U.S. defense obligation was thus limited to Taiwan and the Pescadores—although the treaty allowed for the defense of other territories (i.e., the offshore islands) "as may be determined by mutual agreement."[21] The treaty was signed on December 2, 1954, and ratified by the U.S. Senate on February 9, 1955.

However, after the Communist takeover of the Yijiangshan Islands in early 1955, the United States became concerned that PRC attacks on the offshore islands would be a fatal blow to the morale of ROC troops. While the mutual defense treaty had formalized the American commitment to defend Taiwan and the Pescadores, the omission of the offshore islands seemed to invite attack. Therefore, Eisenhower sought congressional authorization for the use of military force to defend them if he found it to be necessary. Several lawmakers were concerned that a U.S. commitment would incentivize Taiwan to adopt riskier policies that could pull the United States into conflict. As a compromise, the authorization did not include the names of the islands that might be defended.[22] The Formosa Resolution read:

> [T]he President of the United States . . . is authorized to employ the Armed Forces of the United States as he deems necessary for the specific purpose of securing and protecting Formosa and the Pescadores against armed attack, this authority to include the securing and

---

[19] Dwight D. Eisenhower, "Letter from President Eisenhower to British Prime Minister Churchill, January 25, 1955, in U.S. Department of State, Office of the Historian, *Foreign Relations of the United States*, 1955–1957, Vol. 2, Document 41.

[20] Henry, 2022; Stolper, 1985; Cha, 2016.

[21] Mutual Defense Treaty Between the United States and the Republic of China, December 2, 1954.

[22] Pang, 2019.

protection of *such related positions and territories of that area now in friendly hands.*[23]

This more vaguely worded resolution passed Congress with overwhelming support. Thus, while the alliance treaty did not obligate the United States to defend the offshore islands, the Formosa Resolution gave the President the power to do so. The Secretary of State used the resolution to convince Chiang Kai-shek to evacuate the less strategically valuable Dachen Islands, with a private assurance the United States would support the defense of the more valuable Quemoy and Matsu Islands. The ROC sought a public statement from the United States that it would defend Quemoy and Matsu, but Eisenhower refused out of concern that doing so would upset members of Congress and allies—such as Japan and the United Kingdom—that were worried about becoming entrapped in a conflict.[24] The administration also sought to prevent ROC adventurism by making its commitment to Quemoy less than clear.[25] Thus, the U.S. policy of strategic ambiguity—today made in reference to the U.S. commitment to Taiwan as a whole—had its origins in the U.S. position on these offshore islands.[26] The First Taiwan Strait Crisis ended shortly after the passage of the resolution and the ratification of the alliance.[27]

The Second Taiwan Strait crisis erupted in the late summer of 1958, as Beijing once again attacked islands in the Taiwan Strait.[28] During this second

---

[23] Public Law 84-4, Formosa Resolution (Joint Resolution Authorizing the President to Employ the Armed Forces of the United States for Protecting the security of Formosa, the Pescadores and Related Positions and Territories of That Area), January 29, 1955. Emphasis added.

[24] Henry, 2022. Stolper, 1985; Pang, 2019.

[25] Morton H. Halperin, *The 1958 Taiwan Straits Crisis: A Documented History*, RAND Corporation, RM-4900-ISA, 1966.

[26] Bernkopf Tucker, 2011, pp. 1415. See also Thomas C. Schelling, *Arms and Influence*, Yale University Press, 1966, p. 67.

[27] Pang, 2019.

[28] Christensen argues that the crisis was primarily motivated by Mao's desire to distract domestic audiences from the disastrous Great Leap Forward (Thomas J. Christensen, *Useful Adversaries: Grand Strategy, Domestic Mobilization, and Sino-American Conflict, 1947–1958*, Vol. 179, Princeton University Press, 1996). Whiting argues that

crisis, the United States reiterated its position that the Formosa Resolution gave the President authority to defend offshore islands.[29] Despite pleas from Taipei and recommendations from the Pentagon to publicly declare a clear commitment to defend Quemoy, the administration resisted. Concerns about the reaction from Congress and allies in the region—and continuing concerns about incentivizing reckless behavior on the part of the ROC— deterred Eisenhower and Dulles from making such a statement.[30] However, the administration sought to convey its potential willingness to intervene through a military build-up in the area.

While the Formosa Resolution gave Eisenhower the power to defend the offshore islands, this was contingent on Communist attacks being part of an effort to conquer Taiwan. By this line of reasoning, an attack directed solely at these minor islands may have avoided an American response.[31] Mao Zedong was thus surprised when the United States deployed several carriers to the region in response to PRC attacks on Quemoy and Matsu.[32] The crisis ended shortly after it became clear that the United States was willing to defend the islands.

Debate over U.S. policy toward the offshore islands remained prominent in subsequent years and was even highlighted in one of the 1960 presiden-

---

Beijing's desire to test the American commitment toward the "offshore islands" motivated Beijing's escalation (Allen S. Whiting, "New Light on Mao: 3. Quemoy 1958: Mao's Miscalculations," *China Quarterly*, Vol. 62, 1975).

[29] Halperin, 1966, p. 231.

[30] Halperin, 1966.

[31] "Mao deliberately sought to avoid American involvement by putting pressure solely on the Offshore Islands, thereby defusing the joint Congressional resolution of January 1955, which authorized President Dwight D. Eisenhower to intervene with force if he determined that a threat to Taiwan existed" (Whiting, 1975, p. 266). White continues that "all indicators suggested that the immediate target was the Offshore Islands, not Taiwan. No assembly of shipping occurred commensurate with the needs for invasion across the Strait. The increased likelihood of typhoons in September and their continued possibility in October made an invasion extremely" (p. 266).

[32] Whiting, 1975. Others argue that Mao's motivation for starting the crisis was primarily to distract his domestic audience from the disaster of the Great Leap Forward (Christensen, 1996).

tial debates.[33] John F. Kennedy seemed to desire an ROC evacuation from the offshore islands as a senator in 1958[34] and as a presidential candidate in 1960.[35] However, when a near-crisis occurred in 1962, he followed Eisenhower's example of avoiding a specific commitment to the offshore islands while still attempting to convey a willingness to defend them.[36] The ambiguity over U.S. commitment to the Quemoy and Matsu islands thus existed from 1955 until the repeal of the Formosa Resolution in 1974.

Throughout the 1950s and '60s, the United States deployed military forces to Taiwan and provided aid to Nationalist forces. For example, between 1953 and 1973, the United States gave over 1,500 combat aircraft (including advanced fighters) to the ROC and provided training for pilots.[37] The United States also provided support for the construction of air bases on Taiwan, which could be utilized not only by ROC forces but also the U.S. Air Force.[38] At the same time, American strategists were cognizant to avoid giving the ROC too much offensive capability and avoided providing equipment that could be used for "sustained operations on the mainland."[39]

1970s–1980s: U.S.-Taiwan Relations Change; Strategic Ambiguity Is Born

Major geopolitical developments, such as the Sino-Soviet split and the war in Vietnam, led to a change in U.S. strategy by the early 1970s. By the end of the decade, the United States had switched its official recognition of the government of China from Taipei to Beijing, abrogated the alliance with Taiwan, and removed all U.S. forces from the island. Through a series of

---

[33] Stolper, 1985, p. 132.

[34] Halperin, 1966.

[35] Stolper, 1985.

[36] National Archives, "News Conference 37, June 27, 1962," JFK Library, June 27, 1962.

[37] Garver, 1999, pp. 66–67.

[38] Garver, 1999, p. 68.

[39] Garver, 1999, p. 68.

documents and agreements (summarized in Table 2.1), the United States developed what has come to be known as its "One China Policy."[40]

The Shanghai Communiqué

After Richard Nixon took office, National Security Adviser Henry Kissinger secretly traveled to Beijing in 1971, and the President publicly visited Beijing the following year. This meeting led to the first of three communiqués on U.S. relations with Taiwan and the PRC: the 1972 Shanghai Communiqué.[41] In it, the United States acknowledged that "all Chinese on either side of the Taiwan Strait maintain there is but one China and that Taiwan is a part of China." It also stated the United States had an "interest in a peaceful settlement of the Taiwan question by the Chinese themselves" and declared "the ultimate objective of the withdrawal of all U.S. forces and military installations from Taiwan." Full normalization of relations would be delayed, how-

TABLE 2.1

Documents That Define the U.S. One China Policy

Document	Year	Description
The Three Communiqués:		
Shanghai Communiqué	1972	U.S. acknowledges that "all Chinese on either side of the Taiwan Strait maintain there is but one China and that Taiwan is a part of China"
Normalization Communiqué	1978	U.S. recognizes PRC as the legal government of China
Arms Sales Communiqué	1982	U.S. "does not seek to carry out a long-term policy of arms sales to Taiwan"
Taiwan Relations Act	1979	Requires arms of defensive nature be provided to Taiwan
Six Assurances	1982	No definite timeline to arms sales

SOURCE: Information from Bush, 2015.

---

[40] Richard C. Bush, "A One-China Policy Primer," Brookings Institution, East Asia Policy Paper 10, Vol. 10, 2017.

[41] Joint Communiqué of the United States of America and the People's Republic of China Shanghai Communiqué, February 28, 1972.

ever, by the Watergate scandal. Still, the United States took a step toward normalization by repealing the Formosa Resolution in 1974 (the alliance was not terminated until 1979).

The Normalization Communiqué

The Jimmy Carter administration ultimately normalized relations with the PRC. A 1979 communiqué switched U.S. diplomatic recognition from the ROC to the PRC.[42] Normalization not only required that Washington recognize the PRC as the only legitimate government of China, but also that the United States abrogate the alliance with Taipei and remove all U.S. military forces from the island.[43] Accordingly, over the course of the next year the United States dissolved its defense treaty with the ROC and withdrew all its military personal and assets from Taiwan.

The Taiwan Relations Act

Some in Congress supported normalization, arguing that a change in geopolitical circumstances made China a more important partner than Taiwan.[44] However, others in Congress were less supportive of the administration's changes.[45] One reason for their opposition was a belief that abandoning Taiwan would undermine confidence in the U.S. commitment to other regional allies.[46]

Though ultimately unsuccessful, a group of lawmakers led by Senator Barry Goldwater attempted to enjoin the Carter administration from terminating the alliance by arguing that the President did not have authority to withdraw from a treaty.[47] After failing to stop the treaty's abrogation, Con-

---

[42] Joint Communiqué of the United States of America and the People's Republic of China, January 1, 1979.

[43] Bush, 2015, p. 139.

[44] Martin B. Gold, *A Legislative History of the Taiwan Relations Act: Bridging the Strait*, Lexington Books, 2016.

[45] Gold, 2016.

[46] Gold, 2016, pp. 83, 95.

[47] *Goldwater v. Carter*, 444 U.S. 996, 1979.

gress passed the Taiwan Relations Act (TRA) in 1979 to outline U.S. policy toward the island after the change in diplomatic recognition.[48] The TRA includes, among other things, a declaration that the United States would "consider any effort to determine the future of Taiwan by other than peaceful means . . . a threat to the peace and security of the Western Pacific area and of grave concern to the United States," as well as provide Taiwan with defensive weapons and to maintain the capacity to resist any resort to force.[49] Notably, this fell short of the explicit security guarantee the security treaty had provided and was not—like the Formosa Resolution—a formal authorization for the use of military force. While intended to convey support, the lack of an explicit commitment thus inaugurated the U.S. policy of strategic ambiguity toward the defense of Taiwan. Like the policy on offshore islands in the 1950s and '60s, strategic ambiguity here was meant to have dual deterrent purposes. On one hand, the policy was meant to deter the PRC from attacking the island. On the other hand, the lack of an explicit commitment to Taiwan was designed to deter reckless behavior by Taiwan—most specifically, declaring independence.[50]

Strategic ambiguity was not without detractors. One senator opined that the compromise language "does not adequately express what the Nation's policy would be and what the American people would feel should be our policy" and that it would not reassure U.S. regional allies.[51] A committee

---

[48] The administration had proposed its own bill on the future relationship with Taiwan, but Congress rewrote it to address the question of the future security of the island (Gold, 2016). There had been a proposal to deal with the security question alone in a separate bill, but there was a concern Carter would simply veto this independent measure. Wanting to force the President into either vetoing the entire Taiwan bill or accept the security provisions, the Senate intentionally included all Taiwan issues in the TRA (Gold, 2016, p. 82). The original bill proposed by the administration had lacked any security provision, but Congress was adamant that one be included. While some members of Congress had essentially advocated for language creating a security guarantee on par with the soon-to-be defunct Mutual Defense Treaty, the language eventually included in the act was the outcome of a compromise (Gold, 2016, p. 133).

[49] Public Law 96-8, 1979.

[50] For a more recent discussion of this dual deterrence logic, see Bonnie S. Glaser, Michael J. Mazarr, Michael J. Glennon, Richard Haass, and David Sacks, "Dire Straits: Should American Support for Taiwan Be Ambiguous?" *Foreign Affairs*, Vol. 24, 2020.

[51] Gold, 2016, p. 134.

report from the Senate Foreign Relations Committee said that, in the event of an attack on Taiwan, "a United States failure to respond firmly would have grave consequences for America's international standing and would seriously weaken the confidence of America's other allies in the reliability of United States protection."[52]

The Arms Sales Communiqué and the Six Assurances

Arms sales to the island proved to be an irritant in the U.S.-PRC relationship because they continued even after the termination of the U.S.-ROC alliance. Thus, the United States and the PRC issued a third communiqué in 1982 that stated a U.S. intention to decrease arms transfers over time. Also known as the Arms Sales Communiqué, the United States stated that it

> does not seek to carry out a long-term policy of arms sales to Taiwan, that its arms sales to Taiwan will not exceed, either in qualitative or in quantitative terms, the level of those supplied in recent years . . . that it intends to reduce gradually its sales of arms to Taiwan, leading over a period of time to a final resolution.[53]

Soon thereafter, however, pressure from Congress and Taipei led the Ronald Reagan administration to clarify its interpretation of the communiqué via the so-called Six Assurances:

1. The United States would not set a date for termination of arms sales to Taiwan.
2. The United States would not alter the terms of the Taiwan Relations Act.
3. The United States would not consult with China in advance before making decisions about U.S. arms sales to Taiwan.
4. The United States would not mediate between Taiwan and China.

---

[52] Gold, 2016, p. 146.

[53] Joint Communiqué of the United States of America and the People's Republic of China (Arms Sales Communiqué), August 17, 1982.

5. The United States would not alter its position about the sovereignty of Taiwan which was, that the question was one to be decided peacefully by the Chinese themselves and would not pressure Taiwan to enter into negotiations with China.
6. The United States would not formally recognize Chinese sovereignty over Taiwan.[54]

Despite these assurances, the Reagan administration took an overall moderate policy toward Taiwan as it sought to cooperate militarily with China in strategic competition with the Soviet Union.[55] The ROC government became worried about total abandonment in the face of such cooperation, and even restarted its previously shuttered nuclear weapon program in the mid-1980s. Pressure from the Reagan administration ended the program by 1988, however.[56]

Despite differences over Taiwan, and the lack of U.S. clarity on its intentions regarding Taiwan, U.S. and Chinese cooperation reached new heights during the 1980s as both sought to balance against the mutually perceived threat of the Soviet Union.[57] After a series of key events, however, Chinese and American threat perceptions returned once again to mutual suspicion. China's violent response to the 1989 Tiananmen Square protests—and the reaction to it in the West—alongside the stunning American victory in the Gulf War and the collapse of the Soviet Union in 1991, all served as a dramatic "trifecta" that led to a rapid strategic reorientation of both parties.[58]

---

[54] U.S. House of Representatives, "Reaffirming the Taiwan Relations Act and the Six Assurances as Cornerstones of United States-Taiwan Relations," H.Con.Res.88, 2016.

[55] Bernkopf Tucker, 2011, p. 161.

[56] Alexander L. George and Richard Smoke, *Deterrence in American Foreign Policy: Theory and Practice*, Columbia University Press, 1974, p. 163.

[57] Rush Doshi, *The Long Game: China's Grand Strategy and the Displacement of American Order*, Oxford University Press, 2021.

[58] Doshi, 2021.

Post–Cold War Developments: Strategic Ambiguity Under Stress

The end of the Cold War and a domestic backlash in the United States against the PRC following the events in Tiananmen Square led to a distancing of the Sino-American relationship in the early 1990s. Over the course of the next three decades, successive U.S. administrations maintained the policy of strategic ambiguity, although some have been less "ambiguous" than others.

The Third Taiwan Strait Crisis began in 1995 when American lawmakers pressured the White House into allowing Taiwan President Lee Teng-hui to come to the United States to give a speech at his alma mater, Cornell University, even though a 1994 review of Taiwan policy under the William Clinton administration had ruled out such visits. In between Lee's private visit to the United States and Taiwan's presidential election in March of 1996, China conducted a series of military drills that involved firing missiles into the Taiwan Strait. In a March 7, 1995, meeting between Chinese delegates and the U.S. National Security Adviser and Secretaries of Defense and State, the United States characterized the PRC's actions as "reckless" and "an act of coercion."[59] U.S. Secretary of State Warren Christopher reiterated publicly that the United States had conveyed that there would be "grave consequences" if China were to attack Taiwan.[60] Notably, the United States never explicitly declared what it would do if Taiwan were directly attacked. In fact, during the most acute period of the crisis in March 1996, White House Press Secretary Mike McCurry stated the TRA did not specifically answer the question of whether the United States was obligated to intervene militarily on behalf of Taiwan, and that "there is merit . . . in keeping somewhat ambiguous about the answer."[61]

---

[59] John W. Garver, *Face Off: China, the United States, and Taiwan's Democratization*, University of Washington Press, 2011, p. 102.

[60] Garver, 2011, p. 103.

[61] American Presidency Project, "William J. Clinton Press Briefing by Mike McCurry," March 12, 1996.

Despite the White House's efforts to maintain strategic ambiguity, Congress tried to signal greater support. In a resolution, the House of Representatives called for the United States to maintain its capacity to resist any coercion that would "jeopardize the security, or the social or economic system, of the people on Taiwan," to maintain a naval presence in and near the Taiwan Straits, to supply Taiwan with defensive weapons, and to assist in defending Taiwan against invasion, missile attack, or blockade by the PRC.[62] The resolution passed the House in an overwhelmingly bipartisan vote (369–14), although the Senate version used weaker language. Ultimately the crisis abated after Taiwan's presidential election at the end of March 1996.

In the aftermath of the crisis, both the United States and China sought to improve their relationship. In 1998, Clinton announced a policy that would become known as the "Three No's": no support for two Chinas (or one China and one Taiwan), no support for Taiwan's independence, and no support for Taiwan's entry into international organizations that required statehood. China had hoped for a fourth communiqué ending arms sales, but the United States did not offer one.[63] Congress, however, disagreed with these conciliatory efforts and instead sought to boost support for Taiwan. Although the bill failed in the Senate, the House passed the Taiwan Security Enhancement Act (TSEA) in 2000. The act would have mandated U.S. flag-rank officers to travel to Taiwan and permitted the sale of advanced weapon systems. The legislation also would have created a direct communication link between U.S. Pacific Command and Taipei, thus allowing for U.S.-Taiwan interoperability similar to what American forces have with formal treaty allies.[64]

The George W. Bush administration leaned, at least initially, toward more clarity on U.S. policy vis-à-vis Taiwan and adopted many of the measures contained in the TSEA.[65] When asked whether Washington had an

---

[62] U.S. House of Representatives, A Concurrent Resolution Expressing the Sense of Congress Regarding Missile Tests and Military Exercises by the People's Republic of China, Bill 148, March 21, 1996.

[63] Bernkopf Tucker, 2011, p. 234.

[64] Bernkopf Tucker, 2011, p. 246.

[65] For example, only three months into office, the administration announced a major weapons deal, including eight diesel-electric submarines.

obligation to defend Taiwan, Bush responded "Yes, we do, and the Chinese must understand that."[66] When asked whether the United States would use "the full force of the American military" in Taiwan's defense, Bush declared the United States would do "whatever it took to help Taiwan defend herself [sic]."[67] While the White House press secretary argued that Bush's comments were a reiteration of the TRA, others in the administration conceded that Bush was "using stronger language than any previous U.S. leader when it comes to defending Taiwan."[68]

Ultimately, the Bush administration scaled back its positions on Taiwan, resulting in a return toward strategic ambiguity.[69] The 9/11 terrorist attacks shifted U.S. focus to a global campaign against terrorism, and securing PRC support for the War on Terrorism became a paramount concern. Subsequently, Chen Shui-bian, the first ROC president from the more independence-leaning Democratic Progressive Party, took actions seen as provocative toward the PRC without the support of Washington. Most notably, Chen's desire to hold a referendum on Taiwan sovereignty received major pushback from the White House.[70]

The return to strategic ambiguity remained the norm for the next decade and a half. In Taiwan, the Ma Ying-jeou administration, which succeeded the Chen Shui-bian administration in 2008, stabilized relations with the PRC through a series of economic agreements and the institutionalization of diplomatic channels.[71] As concerns about Taiwan's relations with China faded, there was little reason to revisit the policy of strategic ambiguity. Renewed controversy over U.S. policy arrived with the election of Donald Trump in 2016. Then President-Elect Trump caused an uproar in Beijing

---

[66] Joseph R. Biden, Jr., "Not So Deft on Taiwan," *Washington Post*, May 2, 2001.

[67] "Bush Pledges Whatever It Takes to Defend Taiwan," CNN, April 25, 2001.

[68] "Bush Pledges Whatever It Takes to Defend Taiwan," 2001.

[69] Michael D. Swaine, "Taiwan's Management of Relations with the United States During the First Chen Shui-bian Administration," Carnegie Endowment for International Peace, May 5, 2005.

[70] Swaine, 2005.

[71] Yasuhiro Matsuda, "Cross-Strait Relations under the Ma Ying-jeou administration: From Economic to Political Dependence?" *Journal of Contemporary East Asia Studies*, Vol. 4, No. 2, 2015.

when he accepted a congratulatory phone call from Taiwan President Tsai Ing-wen.[72] And prior to inauguration, Trump suggested that he would perhaps alter the One China Policy. Like his predecessors, ultimately Trump did not. He did, however, continue to approve major arms sales to Taiwan, including the sale of M1A2 main battle tanks and F-16 fighters.[73]

U.S. policy continues relatively unchanged with the Joe Biden administration. Like the Trump administration, the Biden administration has pursued strategic competition with China.[74] And like Bush, Biden has caused confusion over U.S. policy by publicly stating (four times as of late 2022) his intention to defend Taiwan against a PRC attack.[75] In keeping with the policy strategic ambiguity, however, the White House and Department of State have sought to walk back Biden's comments by consistently asserting that the United States had not altered its policy toward Taiwan. In Congress, too, there have been efforts to increase support for Taiwan via other means.[76] Some members have, for example, suggested an authorization for the use of military force for the defense of Taiwan (similar to the 1955 Formosa Resolution).[77] The 2023 National Defense Authorization Act reaffirmed Congress's commitment to assist Taiwan in deterring an invasion by the mainland, providing further foreign military financing for Taiwan and establishing a training program to improve interoperability with Tai-

---

[72] Bush, 2017.

[73] Glaser, 2020.

[74] Moreover, Biden's characterization of a worldwide ideological competition between democracies and autocracies had clear applications to cross-strait relations.

[75] "White House Backtracks after Biden Appears to Say US Would Defend Taiwan Against China," *The Guardian*, August 19, 2021; Zolan Kanno-Youngs and Peter Baker, "Biden Pledges to Defend Taiwan if It Faces a Chinese Attack," *New York Times*, May 23, 2022; Kevin Liptak, "Biden Vows to Protect Taiwan in Event of Chinese Attack," CNN, October 22, 2021.

[76] Caitlin Campbell and Susan L. Lawrence, *Taiwan: Political and Security Issues*, Congressional Research Service, 2022.

[77] Elaine Luria, "Congress Must Untie Biden's Hands on Taiwan," *Washington Post*, October 11, 2021.

wan's military.[78] Outside of formal legislation, senior lawmakers have visited Taiwan to convey Congress's support. This gained global attention in August 2022 when U.S. House Speaker Nancy Pelosi, then third in line to the U.S. presidency, visited the island. China responded by conducting large-scale military exercises around Taiwan that included launching missiles over the island, leading some commentators to call it the beginning of the Fourth Taiwan Strait Crisis.[79] In the months following her visit, China has kept up the higher level of day-to-day military activities, such as air patrols, near the island.

Conclusion

Washington's relationship with Taipei has thus varied greatly over time. While the United States briefly experimented with abandoning Nationalist forces on the island in 1949–1950, with the outbreak of the Korean War in June 1950, the United States became actively engaged in the defense of Taiwan from attacks across the Taiwan Strait. By 1955, Washington had ratified a full-fledged alliance with Taipei, although this would come to an end in 1979 with the normalization in relations between the United States and the PRC. Since 1979, Washington has maintained a policy of strategic ambiguity that continues to this day.

Recent U.S. policy suggests that the United States is more likely to continue increasing, rather than decreasing, support to Taiwan in the near term. However, a growing number of questions about U.S. support to international allies and partners among some in Congress raises the possibility that a future U.S. leader could change course.[80] Therefore, in the chapters that follow, we consider how allies would respond to a change in U.S. policy in either direction.

---

[78] Public Law 117-263, U.S. House of Representatives, National Defense Authorization Act for Fiscal Year 2023, December 7, 2022.

[79] Christopher P. Twomey, "The Fourth Taiwan Strait Crisis is Just Starting," *War on the Rocks*, August 22, 2022.

[80] See, for example, Ashley Parker, Marianna Sotomayor, and Isaac Stanley-Becker, "Inside the Republican Drift Away from Supporting the NATO alliance," *Washington Post*, April 29, 2022.

CHAPTER 3

Japan

Japan believes that Beijing's control of Taiwan would deeply affect Japan's security. Moreover, Japan sees U.S. policy toward Taiwan as a signal of U.S. commitment to the region generally and Japan in particular. In this chapter, we argue that these concerns shape Japan's views of hypothetical changes in U.S. policies regarding Taiwan. We find that Japan strongly favors U.S. policies that appear to signal a closer relationship with Taiwan because such policies are thought to both deter attacks on the island and signal a stronger commitment to the region. Conversely, Tokyo would be concerned if the United States were to pursue policies that downgrade ties with Taiwan.

History of Japan's Relations with Taiwan

Japan colonized Taiwan in 1895 out of a desire to expand its imperial footprint, as well as a fear that the island could be used by Western countries to invade Japan's southwestern islands.[1] Japan controlled the island until its defeat in World War II. Following the end of the U.S. occupation of Japan in 1952, Japanese leadership followed the United States in choosing to maintain diplomatic relations with the ROC rather than with the PRC. Contemporary Japanese leadership understood, however, that for Japan to recover after the war, trade with mainland China was critical.[2] Despite a desire to remain flexible toward the PRC, Japanese leadership recognized the ROC

---

[1] Seiji Shirane, "Imperial Gateway: Colonial Taiwan and Japan's Expansion in South China and Southeast Asia, 1895–1945," *Asia-Pacific Journal*, Vol. 20, No. 17, 2022, pp. 2, 5.

[2] Shigeru Yoshida, "Japan and the Crisis in Asia," *Foreign Affairs*, No. 29, 1951, p. 179.

under U.S. pressure. This decision marked the beginning of what one Japanese scholar calls Japan's de facto "two Chinas" policy of increasing contact with Beijing without sacrificing relations with Taipei.[3]

Japan was surprised when the United States pursued rapprochement with China in the 1970s. President Richard Nixon's official visit to the PRC is referred to as the "Nixon Shock" among Japanese historians and policymakers because Tokyo was not consulted on the policy shift. The United States informed the Japanese ambassador to Washington, Ushiba Nobuhiko, of Nixon's announcement less than an hour before it occurred, and the Japanese prime minister, Sato Eisaku, is said to have learned of it only a few minutes before.[4] Tokyo was irritated by this secrecy because it was Washington's influence that had kept Tokyo from improving its relations with Beijing for decades.[5] Japan rapidly moved toward normalization with China, which it did by September 1972. This, in turn, meant relegating Japan-Taiwan relations to a nongovernmental, working-level basis. Japan established a de facto embassy in Taipei—called the Interchange Association—and Taipei did the same in Tokyo. For decades, bilateral relations with Taiwan remained relatively stable, albeit unofficial and always derivative of Japan's China policy.[6]

Officially, Japan seeks "peace and stability in the Taiwan Strait."[7] Although Japan still maintains only unofficial relations with Taiwan, in recent years Tokyo has strengthened these ties with Taipei. For example, in 2011, Japan and Taiwan made a private investment arrangement to bolster financial ties. That same year, they also agreed to an Open Skies Arrangement to make it easier to establish new travel routes between them, fostering more tourism and business travel. And in April 2013, after three decades of stalled negotiations, Japan and Taiwan set aside disagreements about sover-

---

[3] Yoshihide Soeya, "Taiwan in Japan's Security Considerations," *China Quarterly*, No. 165, March 1, 2001.

[4] Soeya, 2001, p. 138.

[5] Sadako Ogata, *Normalization with China: A Comparative Study of U.S. and Japanese Processes*, Institute of East Asian Studies, University of California, 1988, p. 37.

[6] Jeffrey W. Hornung, "Strong but Constrained Japan-Taiwan Ties," Brookings, March 13, 2018.

[7] Ministry of Foreign Affairs (Japan), *Diplomatic Bluebook 2022*, 2022, p. 43.

eignty over the Senkaku Islands to conclude a fishery agreement.[8] Shortly after Tsai Ing-Wen was elected president in 2016, Japanese Prime Minister Abe Shinzō sent an unprecedented congratulatory message, marking the first time a senior Japanese official issued such messages to a president-elect of Taiwan.[9] In January 2017, much to the chagrin of Beijing, Japan changed the name of its Interchange Association to the Japan-Taiwan Exchange Association to explicitly reflect the organization's role in Taiwan (Taiwan's counterpart also changed its name to the Taiwan-Japan Relations Association). A few months later, Japan sent the vice minister of the Ministry of Internal Affairs and Communications to Taiwan to attend a tourism event in his official capacity, marking the highest-level official visit by a government official since 1972.[10] Most recently, Japan provided vaccines to Taipei during the coronavirus 2019 pandemic.[11]

Historically, Japan has refrained from involvement in international disputes and openly criticizing China. Given its proximity to the island and increases in China's military activities in the past decade, concerns about how a war would affect Japan have been growing. Since 2020, there has been a marked increase in the number of references to Taiwan by Japanese politicians. In December of that year, then–State Minister for Defense Nakayama Yasuhide referred to Taiwan as a "red line" during an online event.[12] Despite making this comment in a personal capacity, subsequent statements by other policymakers suggest a growing openness to talk about Taiwan publicly in Japan. For example, numerous statements throughout 2021, including a joint statement by senior U.S. and Japanese officials, included reference to

---

[8]   Ministry of Foreign Affairs (Republic of China), "Republic of China (Taiwan) Signs Fisheries Agreement with Japan," press release, 2020.

[9]   "Abe Congratulates Tsai on Election as Taiwan's President," *Japan Times*, January 18, 2016.

[10]   Reuters, "China Complains After Japanese Minister Visits Taiwan," *Newsweek*, March 27, 2017.

[11]   Ministry of Foreign Affairs (Japan), 2022, p. 6.

[12]   Ju-min Park, "Japan Official, Calling Taiwan 'Red Line,' Urges Biden to 'Be Strong,'" Reuters, December 25, 2020a.

the "importance of peace and stability" in the Taiwan Strait.[13] Further, for the first time since 1969, a joint statement by the U.S. president and Japanese prime minister noted "the importance of peace and stability across the Taiwan Strait" and "peaceful resolution of cross-strait issues."[14] Subsequent joint statements by leaders and officials continue to use the same language.[15] Two of the more attention-grabbing statements were from former prime ministers, in their private capacity. Asō Tarō, at a private fundraising event in July 2021, said that "If a major problem occurred on Taiwan, it is not too much to say that it would unmistakably relate to a situation threatening [Japan's] survival. Japan and the U.S. must defend Taiwan together."[16] A few months later, Abe Shinzō said that a Taiwan contingency is a Japanese contingency, and therefore a contingency for the alliance.[17]

Some analysts see these comments as a signal Japan is willing to defend Taiwan.[18] After all, Japan says that the "stability of the situation surrounding Taiwan" is important for its security.[19] However, there has not been an official change to Japan's policy on Taiwan, the Taiwan Strait issue, or Japan's role in a Taiwan contingency. Like the United States, Japan officially retains

[13] "U.S.- Japan Joint Leaders' Statement: U.S.-Japan Global Partnership for a New Era," April 16, 2021.

[14] "U.S.- Japan Joint Leaders' Statement: U.S.-Japan Global Partnership for a New Era," 2021.

[15] "Joint Statement of the United States and Japan," January 13, 2023; U.S. Embassy and Consulates in Japan, "Joint Statement of the Security Consultative Committee (2+2)," January 11, 2023.

[16] "Possibility of Taiwan Emergency 'Existence Crisis Situation' Deputy Prime Minister Aso [「"台湾有事「存立危機事態」にあたる可能性" 麻生副総理」]," *NHK*, 2021.

[17] Abe Shinzō, "Keynote Speech/Impact Forum" ["キーノートスピーチ / インパクト・フォーラム"], Institute for National Policy Research [國策研究院], video, December 1, 2021.

[18] Ryan Ashley, "Japan's Revolution on Taiwan Affairs," *War on the Rocks*, 2021.

[19] Ministry of Defense (Japan), *Defense of Japan*, 2022a, p. 11.

a policy of strategic ambiguity.[20] And Japanese leaders continue to advocate for disputes over Taiwan's status to be settled peacefully through dialogue.[21]

Relations with China and the United States: Alignment with the United States

Although Japan maintains significant trade ties with China, Tokyo prioritizes its security relations with the United States. Tokyo also shares Washington's view of the challenge that China poses and the necessity to maintain robust alliance ties.

China

Japan's views on regional security align with those of the United States. Japan's historical security challenge was the Soviet Union and later Russia. Over the past 20 years, those concerns have been displaced by concerns about an increasingly powerful China engaging in more assertive behavior in the region, including near Japanese territory. For example, Japan's revised National Security Strategy, released in December 2022, calls China's "current external stance, military activities, and other activities" a matter of "serious concern for Japan" that represent "the greatest strategic challenge in ensuring the peace and security of Japan and the peace and stability of the international community, as well as in strengthening the international order based on the rule of law."[22] Its National Defense Strategy uses similar language, calling out China's efforts "to advance its unilateral changes to the status quo by force" in the East and South China Seas.[23] The Ministry of

---

[20] Adam P. Liff, "Has Japan's Policy Toward the Taiwan Strait Changed?" *Washington Post*, August 18, 2021.

[21] Ministry of Defense (Japan), 2022a, p. 68.

[22] Government of Japan, *National Security Strategy of Japan*, Tokyo, provisional translation, December 16, 2022b, p. 9.

[23] Ministry of Defense (Japan), 2022a, p. 31; Ministry of Foreign Affairs (Japan), 2022, p. 42.

Defense's 2022 *Defense of Japan*, Japan's primary annual defense document, notes with concern that China's power is growing and China is increasingly willing to "change the status quo by coercion."[24] These statements align with those found in U.S. strategic documents, such as the October 2022 U.S. National Security Strategy, which identifies China as the most significant long-term challenge to the United States, and the National Defense Strategy, which calls China the overall pacing challenge for U.S. defense planners.[25]

Specifically, Japan is concerned about China's willingness to use force to exert its claim over the Senkaku Islands, which are administratively controlled by Japan, and to exert control over areas of the East and South China Seas. Japan is also concerned about China's suppression of democracy in Hong Kong and human rights abuses in Xinjiang.[26] Chinese military air and naval activities in and around Japanese territorial waters and airspace only serve to intensify concerns about the threat China could pose to Japanese territory.[27] Growing concern about a Chinese invasion of Taiwan stokes those fears, prompting Japan over the past decade to shift its entire defense strategy to focus on defending its southwestern flank from possible Chinese aggression.[28]

This does not mean that other perspectives on China do not exist. There are some in the business community, for example, that look to China as a business opportunity. This perspective is reflected in a statement by Keizai Doyukai Vice Chair Koshiba Mitsunobu, who said:

---

[24] Ministry of Defense (Japan), 2022a, p. 31; Ministry of Foreign Affairs (Japan), 2022, p. 42.

[25] The White House, 2022, p. 10; U.S. Department of Defense, 2022.

[26] Ministry of Foreign Affairs (Japan), 2022, pp. 43, 45–48. See also Japan's *National Defense Strategy* (NDS), which uses similar language, calling out China's efforts "to advance its unilateral changes to the status quo by force" in the East and South China Seas. (Government of Japan, *National Defense Strategy*, translated by Ministry of Defense of Japan [provisional translation as of December 28, 2022], December 16, 2022a, p. 3.)

[27] Ministry of Defense (Japan), 2022a, p. 42; Ministry of Foreign Affairs (Japan), 2022, pp. 45-50.

[28] Jeffrey W. Hornung, *Japan's Potential Contributions in an East China Sea Contingency*, RAND Corporation, RR-A34-1, 2020.

A comprehensive perspective should be taken in thinking about how Japan should deal with China. Over the course of history, the world's hegemon has changed from the Netherlands to the UK to the U.S., and now China is up for the challenge. . . . We are at a major turning point in world history. . . . Japanese companies should not make a hasty decision to withdraw from China.[29]

China, of course, remains a significant trade partner for Japan, with 26 percent of imports arising from China and 21 percent of its exports going to China. By comparison, 11 percent of Japan's imports arise from the United States, and 18 percent of its exports go to the United States.[30] Likewise, the Liberal Democratic Party's coalition partner, the New Komeito, is considered a friendly bridge for Japan-China relations when bilateral ties get difficult and a brake internally on preventing the Liberal Democratic Party from taking an overly harsh approach to China.[31]

But these perspectives are in the minority today. Even those who manage China relations within the Ministry of Foreign Affairs, which historically has promoted a more cooperative approach toward China, told us that they worry about the threat China poses. Importantly, the critical views of China are supported by the public. According to Cabinet Office polls, ever since 2001, a majority of Japanese citizens have viewed China negatively (e.g., not having an affinity for it).[32] In the most recent poll (2022), the percentage of Japanese who do not have an affinity for China remains high, at 81.8 per-

[29] "Special Issue: 50 Years of Japan-China: Prospects for the Future" ["論点スペシャル] 日中50年　将来を展望"], *Yomiuri Shimbun*, September 29, 2022, p. 14.

[30] Observatory of Economic Complexity, "Japan," undated-a.

[31] "Komeito Head Yamaguchi Seeks to Visit China in January and Build Bridges, Some in Ruling Party Object" ["公明・山口代表、1月の中国訪問模索　橋渡し狙い、与党内で異論も"], *Mainichi Shimbun*, December 22, 2022; Tobias Harris and Levi McLaughlin, "The Small Pacifist Party That Could Shape Japan's Future," *Foreign Policy*, November 4, 2021; Chida Koya, "Komeito Seals Its 'Pro-China' Image, Takes Pride in Its Role as Bridge-Builder While Criticizing an Exercise" ["公明「親中」イメージ封印　橋渡し役自負も演習は批判"], *Sankei Shimbun*, August 17, 2022.

[32] See the China sections in the Government Public Relations Cabinet Office (Japan), "Public Poll on Diplomacy" ["外交に関する世論調査"], 2003–2023.

cent.[33] Collectively, while there may be some pockets of support for milder China policies, the overarching consensus in both government and society is that a harder pushback of China is needed.

United States

Concerns over Chinese behavior have reinforced the view that Japan's alliance with the United States, is the "cornerstone" of Japan's national security policy and broader regional stability.[34] According to one interviewee, the alliance is Japan's most important relationship. As a result, Tokyo has been strengthening ties with the United States. This has included continual evolution in alliance roles and missions (i.e., 2015 U.S.-Japan defense guidelines, expanding Article 5 of the security treaty to include space) to make the alliance more robust. It also has included welcoming new U.S. military forces in Japan (i.e., two Army Navy/Transportable Radar Surveillance systems, temporary deployment of the MQ-9 unmanned aerial vehicle; construction of joint facilities on the uninhabited island of Mageshima; agreeing on a U.S. Marine Littoral Regiment in Okinawa). Importantly, Japan has been tightening its security relationships with other U.S. allies and like-minded partners (i.e., NATO members, Australia, the Philippines) bilaterally[35] and through multilateral institutions, such as the Quadrilateral Security Dialogue, better known as the Quad, contributing to what a RAND report called a "thickening web" of security cooperation.[36]

The culmination of Japan's efforts came in its strategic documents released in December 2022. The National Security Strategy described the U.S.-Japan alliance as playing "an indispensable role not only for the secu-

---

[33] Government Public Relations Cabinet Office (Japan), "Japan and China" ["日本と中国"], "Summary of the Public Poll on Diplomacy" ["外交に関する世論調査 の概要"], February 13, 2023.

[34] Government of Japan, 2022b, p. 5.

[35] Jeffrey W. Hornung, "Abe Shinzō's Lasting Impact: Proactive Contributions to Japan's Security and Foreign Policies," *Asia-Pacific Review*, Vol. 28, No. 1, 2021.

[36] Scott W. Harold et al., *The Thickening Web of Asian Security Cooperation: Deepening Defense Ties Among U.S. Allies and Partners in the Indo-Pacific*, RAND Corporation, RR-3125-MCF, 2019; Mari Yamaguchi, "Japan, Philippines Agree to Sharply Boost Defense Ties," AP News, February 9, 2023.

rity of Japan but also for the realization of peace and stability in the international community."[37] The document goes on to describe Japan's efforts to build and expand a multilayered network with the United States and other like-minded countries to strengthen deterrence.[38] Toward that end, Japan's new National Defense Strategy and accompanying Defense Buildup Plan outline plans to invest in new capabilities to better cooperate with the United States to achieve the shared objective of deterring China from using coercion and force in the region to unilaterally overturn the status quo.[39]

Alliance politics can be complicated by fears of entanglement (i.e., being pulled into war by an ally) and abandonment (i.e., the loss of allied support).[40] For example, during the Gulf War and Iraq War, some in Japan feared that the United States would entangle Japan in adventures unrelated to Japanese interests.[41] Occasionally this view is prevalent in the local politics of Okinawa, as well, which is home to 70.4 percent of areas exclusively used by U.S. forces stationed in Japan, despite the prefecture only amounting to 0.6 percent of Japan's total land area.[42] Occasionally hints of abandonment fears crop up, such as a 2020 editorial calling for the United States to take a strong stand against China to reassure Japan and other partners about its commitment, but these do not appear to be the majority sentiment in Tokyo.[43] However, neither abandonment nor entanglement concerns play a strong role in the U.S.-Japan alliance today due to overarching alignment over shared security concerns. Japan often takes the lead on regional initiatives, such as the Quad or the Free and Open Indo-Pacific initiative, with

---

[37] Government of Japan, 2022b, p. 12.

[38] Government of Japan, 2022b, p. 13.

[39] Ministry of Defense (Japan), *Defense Buildup Plan* ["「防 衛 力 整 備 計 画」"], December 16, 2022b.

[40] Glenn H. Snyder, *Alliance Politics*, Cornell University Press, 1997.

[41] Jeffrey W. Hornung, *Learning How to Sweat: Explaining the Dispatch of Japan's Self-Defense Forces in the Gulf War and Iraq War*, Columbian College of Arts and Sciences of the George Washington University, dissertation, UMI No. 3366728, August 31, 2009.

[42] Okinawa Prefectural Government, "What Okinawa Wants You to Understand About the U.S. Military Bases," March 1, 2018, p. 2.

[43] "The Virtues of a Confrontational China Strategy," *American Interest*, April 10, 2020.

close coordination with the United States, but this stems more from Japan's growing confidence and reemergence as a geopolitical actor, not out of fear of U.S. abandonment or prodding.[44]

View of Taiwan: Directly Linked to Japan's Security

Historically, Japan did not publicly speak about the linkages between Taiwan and Japan's own security, but that appears to be changing. Mentions of Taiwan have been increasing in both official and unofficial statements, as noted above. Japan's December 2022 National Security Strategy describes Taiwan as "an extremely important partner and a precious friend of Japan, with whom Japan shares fundamental values, including democracy, and has close economic and personal ties." The document also describes the peace and stability of the Taiwan Strait as being "an indispensable element for the security and prosperity of the international community."[45] Japan's National Defense Strategy states that Japan has security concerns about China's coercive military activities around Taiwan.[46] As one respondent noted, "A Taiwan crisis is a Japan crisis." Several respondents echoed this sentiment, noting that Japanese territory near Taiwan would likely be engulfed in a war should conflict break out in the Taiwan Strait.

Given this connection, there is broad consensus in Japan that U.S. policies on Taiwan strongly affect Japan. As one interviewee characterized it, Japan's approach to Taiwan is "100% affected by the U.S." A separate respondent commented that "every single change in U.S. policy may affect Japan's future." Many people we interviewed cited the historic example of Japan's desire to recognize the PRC in 1949 but, under U.S. pressure, Japan recognized the ROC instead. Similarly, it was only after Kissinger visited China and began to downgrade relations with Taiwan that Japan followed suit. Japan still largely follows the U.S. lead, but rather than the U.S. pressuring Japan, interviewees noted that Japan "very closely" watches U.S. actions.

---

[44] Jeffrey W. Hornung, "Japan's Long-Awaited Return to Geopolitics," *Foreign Policy,* February 6, 2023.

[45] Government of Japan, 2022b, p. 14.

[46] Government of Japan, 2022a, p. 6.

Because of the connections between U.S. policy on Taiwan and its implications for Japan, Tokyo regularly consults and coordinates with Washington on issues related to Taiwan. After all, according to all interviewees in Japan, the proximity of Taiwan to Japanese territory means that a crisis involving Taiwan will inevitability affect Japan.

Although Japan tends to follow U.S. policy on Taiwan, Japan is still limited on what it can do. One interviewee explained that Japan does not have the legal basis or political support to supply Taiwan with arms the way the United States does. Similarly, Japan does not see itself as in a position to initiate new policies or take the lead on changes to Taiwan policy. It does, however, see itself as "supporting activities of the U.S. that could support Taiwan." That said, several respondents argued that the more forward leaning the United States is with Taiwan, the more Japan can follow in its initiatives with Taiwan.

Japan's view of the connections between Taiwan and Japan's interests can be seen in their interpretation of recent U.S. actions. Interviewees generally supported Biden's statements that the United States would defend Taiwan, which they believed would reduce the risk of war by reducing the possibility of China's miscalculations about U.S. commitment to Taiwan. Most interviewees reasoned that Biden's statements were deliberate, meant to probe how the PRC would respond. For these people, Biden's statements were a welcome development because they give Taiwan confidence that it is not alone and make China less likely to attack Taiwan which, in turn, makes Japan "feel more secure." That said, subsequent corrections by the State Department or White House did give some respondents a cause for concern because it sent a confused message to regional allies about the direction of U.S. policy. Respondents did not agree on whether these collective statements were good or bad for Japan's security, but they did not interpret these U.S. actions as disrupting the status quo.

Japan also saw its security affected by Nancy Pelosi's visit to Taiwan in August 2022. Most interviewees had concerns about the visit, both the timing and its intended objective. In addition to some viewing the visit as serving her own domestic political purposes and concerns over the timing of the visit so close to China's 20th Party Congress, interviewees worried that the visit provided China "leeway" to create "new standards" for how to respond; in other words, giving China an excuse to potentially create a new normal of more-assertive military activities. Because Japan's interest is to maintain peace and stability in the Taiwan Strait, the United States needs to be careful not to give China an excuse to change the status quo. Once China increases military activities, interviewees argued, it tends to maintain those changes, which adversely affect Japan and its security.

Despite the United States not having a treaty alliance with Taiwan, Japanese respondents said that U.S. policies toward Taiwan send a signal about the U.S. commitment to Japan. If the U.S. cannot or will not defend Taiwan against China, interviewees explained, Japan will ask whether there are other territories that are not considered strategically important for the United States to defend against China, such as the Senkaku Islands. "If we lose Taiwan," according to one individual, "we lose the alliance" with the United States, because Japan's ability to look at the United States as a reliable security guarantee will cease to exist.

While interviewees support U.S. criticisms of coercive Chinese actions, respondents also want those words to be backed up by U.S. action. As one respondent put it, both "words and deeds" are important for deterrence to work. As another interviewee explained, "Power is the only language the PRC understands." A third individual said that if the United States responds to Chinese aggression through diplomatic statements, "that is the worst-case scenario" for Japan. While there was no interest in the United States overwhelmingly pushing back on China, those we spoke with wanted the United States to ensure its responses are proportionate to the PRC's action, thereby favoring U.S. pushback against China. The consensus among interviewees was that the United States providing such proportionate pushback will help deter China from attacking Taiwan and others in the region, including Japan. The key point, however, as one respondent noted, is that the United States needs to be prepared to follow through on what it says.

Japanese Views of Hypothetical Changes in U.S. Taiwan Policy

Interviewees in Japan frequently began discussions about hypothetical U.S. policy changes by stating that the two countries closely collaborate on regional policy. Therefore, respondents expected that the United States would discuss any proposed changes in policy toward Taiwan with Japan before making a change.

When asked about hypothetical future U.S. policies to strengthen economic relations with Taiwan, interviewees uniformly supported certain policy ideas. For example, they approved of the idea of U.S. support for Taiwan's membership in regional economic organizations. This included the Asia-Pacific Economic Cooperation, which Japan already supports, and membership of the Comprehensive and Progressive Agreement for Trans-Pacific Partnership (CPTPP), noting that its membership should be approved before the PRC's membership.

Interviewees took a neutral view toward the idea of the United States establishing and/or strengthening intelligence sharing with Taiwan. Respondents stated that intelligence sharing is a bilateral issue between Taiwan and the United States and not of particular concern for Japan.

Views of hypothetical U.S. diplomatic and military policy changes were more varied. Consider, first, diplomatic policies. All interviewees expressed strong support for the United States to use diplomacy to signal a stronger U.S. relationship with Taiwan. For example, interviewees approved of increasing U.S. support for Taiwan's participation in international bodies that do not require statehood for membership, something Japan has already done in the past.[47] The respondents also approved of increasing the number of U.S. public statements warning China against attacking Taiwan. Interviewees saw such statements as promoting peace by deterring China from making miscalculated steps regarding Taiwan. Interviewees also support the idea of more joint statements between the United States and regional allies and partners in diplomatic support of Taiwan. This is because Japan wants to see a larger coalition in support of Taiwan. As one interviewee put it, "We don't want to face China alone." That said, mirroring the comments above about Biden's statements and Pelosi's visit, interviewees wanted the United States to consult with Japan, given that statements could affect the likelihood of war and that any conflict could directly affect Japan's security. Interviewees did not raise the concern held by some U.S. strategists

---

[47] For example, Japan's official Diplomatic Bluebook states that the government has "consistently supported Taiwan's participation as an observer to the WHO General Assembly" (Ministry of Foreign Affairs [Japan], 2022, p. 50).

that these actions would embolden Taiwan to declare independence or take other steps that could increase tensions with China.

Interviewees indicated conditional support for more-explicit U.S. declarations of intent to come to Taiwan's defense and increase official visits. Some interviewees noted that Japan would want the United States to use official visits to promote substantive interactions that serve a greater strategic purpose, not just increase the number of visits for the sake of more visits. Interviewees anticipated that Japan may publicly support future U.S. statements regarding Taiwan's defense, but only after the United States does so. Interviewees also expected China to increase its military activities in the region in response to such statements and worried about such activities going unchecked. Therefore, interviewees would only support an explicit U.S. security guarantee if the U.S. military would be prepared to counter any Chinese military responses. For them, if China becomes more active and the United States does nothing, that is worse than the U.S. not having made the statement in the first place.

Interviewees universally opposed hypothetical U.S. diplomatic actions intended to signal a weakening of U.S. support to Taiwan. This is because interviewees view a weakening of U.S. commitment to Taiwan as a signal of weakening of U.S. commitment to its allies in the region, including Japan. Because the United States is currently engaging in efforts to signal stronger support of Taiwan in the diplomatic domain, several interviewees said the Japanese government would be shocked by policies that would represent a U.S. reversal and would privately oppose a change, pushing Washington to reverse course. One interviewee went as far as to say that such a reversal in its policies would make Japan feel like it cannot rely on the alliance or U.S. commitment any longer. Interviewees did not say what policy changes Japan might undertake in response to such abandonment concerns.

As in the diplomatic domain, Japanese interviewees tended to widely support efforts by the United States that signal a stronger support of Taiwan through changes in military policies. Increasing U.S. arms sales to Taiwan, for example, would be strongly supported because a stronger Taiwan defense is a positive development both for Taiwan and any broader regional contingency that could potentially involve Japan. That support, however, would not be public, as interviewees expressed concern that any public support of increased arms sales could elicit a negative Chinese response against Japan.

Interviewees did say, however, that Japan would be vocally supportive of an increased U.S. presence in the region because it would be a strong sign of U.S. commitment to the region and enhance existing deterrence efforts, both of which are in Japan's interests.[48] The one area where interviewees demonstrated a notable difference of opinion was in U.S. efforts to increase military presence in or around Taiwan. While some saw this as a positive signal in the long term, others were concerned more about short-term effects because increased U.S. presence could signal that the U.S. is preparing for an "imminent" crisis or could trigger a conflict if China feels forced to respond. While no one expressed opposition, there was an expectation that the United States would craft such a strategy closely with Japan, given that its security could be adversely affected by a sudden increase in U.S. military presence on Taiwan.

When asked about military actions that signal a weakening of U.S. support to Taiwan, interviewees universally opposed such actions. Here, too, the reasoning offered by interviewees was that a weakening of U.S. commitment to Taiwan portends a weakening of U.S. commitment to Japan and the broader region. One interviewee noted that a reduction of arms sales to Taiwan would make Japan feel "very insecure," and another said that a reduction in U.S. regional presence would signal that the United States has "given up [its] hegemonic status," which would not be good for Japan. And despite the concern of an increased U.S. military presence on Taiwan, interviewees similarly expressed concern if the United States began to weaken its limited military presence on Taiwan, signaling the status quo as the most desirable state.

It is not clear how Japan's policies would change if the United States were to reduce its support to Taiwan over Japan's objections. Interviewees were highly skeptical that the United States would adopt such a policy, so did not explicitly discuss how Japan's behavior would change in such a situation. However, we can infer Japan's possible responses based on its strategic setting and Japan's orientation toward China and the U.S. alliance gener-

---

[48] This is consistent with sentiments expressed by Japanese participants in a recent dialogue among experts and former officials from the United States, Japan, and Taiwan (Jacques deLisle, *U.S.-Japan-Taiwan Dialogue: Deterrence, Defense, and Trilateral Cooperation*, Foreign Policy Research Institute, December 12, 2022).

ally. Interviews and leaders' statements reveal that Japan has deep insecurity about Chinese power and mistrust of its intentions. Moreover, the U.S. alliance is core to Japan's approach to countering the challenge that China poses. As a result, if the United States were to reduce its support to Taiwan, Japan would likely try to reestablish a common plan for the region with the United States, bind the United States closer to Japan, and continue its efforts to internally balance through increased defense spending.

Conclusion

Japanese views on U.S. policies vis-à-vis Taiwan are best characterized as all-in, with a strong consensus view that Taiwan matters for Japan's security. Any weakening of the U.S. relationship with Taiwan potentially jeopardizes that. Therefore, Japanese respondents both supported the United States engaging Taiwan in the economic and intelligence domains and in signaling a strong commitment to Taiwan by pushing back on any undue Chinese activities in the region that seek to change the status quo. Ultimately, while our interviews suggested that Japan strongly supports U.S. efforts in various diplomatic and military policies (Tables 3.1 and 3.2), respondents made it clear that Japan would want the United States to consult it on any policy change.

TABLE 3.1

Japan's Perspective on U.S. Options for Increasing Support to Taiwan

	U.S. Policy Option	Japan's Perspective
Diplomatic	Advocate for Taiwan's inclusion in fora that do not require statehood	Support
	Increase warnings directed at China about the costs of attacking Taiwan	Support
	Increase emphasis on Taiwan in joint statements	Support
	Increase high-level official interactions	Support
	Explicitly state that the United States will defend Taiwan	Mixed feelings
Military	Increase regional presence	Support
	Increase arms sales and security assistance to Taiwan	Support
	Increase U.S. presence in or near Taiwan	Mixed feelings
	Pursue a bilateral free trade agreement	Support
	Support Taiwan's inclusion in regional trade agreements	Support
	Increased intelligence sharing	Neutral

TABLE 3.2

Japan's Perspective on U.S. Options for Decreasing Support to Taiwan

	U.S. Policy Option	Japan's Perspective
Diplomatic	Decrease high-level official interactions (e.g., Cabinet or senior congressional leaders)	Does not support
	Decrease warnings to China about the costs of attacking Taiwan	Does not support
	Decrease emphasis on Taiwan in joint statements	Does not support
	Explicitly state that the United States will not defend Taiwan	Does not support
Military	Decrease regional presence	Does not support
	Decrease arms sales and security assistance	Does not support
	Decrease U.S. presence in or near Taiwan	Does not support
Economic and information	Reduce economic ties	Does not support
	Increased intelligence sharing	Neutral

CHAPTER 4

The Republic of Korea

The ROK's contemporary Taiwan policy is largely a function of the ROK's attempts to manage relations with both the United States and China. South Korea seeks to strike a delicate balance between supporting the position of the United States, its longtime security ally, and avoiding tensions with China, its major economic partner and an actor considered to have significant influence over South Korea's primary security threat, North Korea. Consistent with this view, South Korea prefers that U.S. policy vis-à-vis Taiwan enhances regional deterrence without unnecessarily provoking a PRC response.

History of South Korea's Relations with Taiwan

Historically, the ROK had strong relations with Taiwan. When the ROK declared statehood in 1948, the ROC was the second nation, after the United States, to officially recognize it.[1] When the government of the ROC fled from mainland China to Taiwan in 1949, the ROK became the first nation to officially recognize this government and move its embassy to Taipei.[2] During the Korean War, Taiwan assisted South Korea.[3] During the Cold War, the ROK and Taiwan collaborated closely on an anti-Communist agenda bilat-

---

[1] Seong-Hyon Lee, "South Korean Angle on the Taiwan Strait: Familiar Issue, Unfamiliar Option," Stimson Center, policy memo, February 23, 2022b.

[2] Junghyun Park, "Frustrated Alignment: The Pacific Pact Proposals from 1949 to 1954 and South Korea–Taiwan Relations," *International Journal of Asian Studies*, Vol. 12, No. 2, 2015.

[3] Lee, 2022b.

erally as well as multilaterally, recognizing the similarity of their circumstances. Seoul and Taipei even considered forming an alliance before each signed separate treaty alliances with the United States.[4]

During the Cold War, South Korea saw U.S. policy toward Taiwan as an indicator of the U.S. commitment to the ROK. This may have been because of the parallels between the situations Taiwan and South Korea faced. Each had an authoritarian, pro-West government standing in opposition to a Communist rival seeking to unify the country by force. During the period when the United States began to normalize relations with the PRC, South Korea worried about U.S. abandonment.[5] This was due, in part, to the end of the commitment to Taiwan, but also the Nixon Doctrine and reduction of forces on the Korean Peninsula.[6] South Korea saw these policies collectively as evidence of a softened U.S. anti-Communist stance and reduced U.S. willingness to defend South Korea from an attack by North Korea.[7] In response to concerns about the U.S. commitment, South Korea sought other ways to provide for its security. Most notably, ROK President Park Chunghee authorized a program to develop nuclear weapons.[8] Seoul suspended the program only because of U.S. pressure and the need to maintain U.S. economic and military support.[9]

As a result, South Korea's policy toward Taiwan has not always mirrored that of the United States. South Korea maintained formal diplomatic ties with Taiwan significantly longer than other U.S. allies and partners. The normalization of diplomatic relations between the ROK and PRC occurred on August 24, 1992, two decades after Nixon's visit to China and 13 years after the United States formally recognized the PRC. In part, this delay was

---

[4] Park, 2015.

[5] Seung-Young Kim, "Nationalism and the Pursuit of Nuclear Weapons and Missiles: The South Korean Case, 1970–82," *Diplomacy & Statecraft*, Vol. 12, No. 4, 2001.

[6] Kim, 2001.

[7] Leon Whyte, "Evolution of the U.S.-ROK Alliance: Abandonment Fears," *The Diplomat*, June 22, 2015; Don Oberdorfer and Robert Carlin, *The Two Koreas: A Contemporary History*, Basic Books, 1997; Kim, 2001, p. 11.

[8] National Foreign Assessment Center, "South Korea: Nuclear Developments and Strategic Decisionmaking," declassified for release, October 2005, June 1, 1978.

[9] Kim, 2001.

due to Beijing's reluctance to have closer ties with South Korea for fear that formally recognizing the existence of two Koreas might undermine its own One China policy, concerns that dissipated when both South Korea and North Korea were officially admitted to the United Nations.[10] By this time, it had become clear to the ROK that recognition of the PRC would provide both enhanced economic cooperation and provide South Korea with a more cooperative relationship with the only nation who might provide a check on North Korea's behavior, paving the way for normalization.[11]

The switch in ROK recognition from Taipei to Beijing was a surprise for leadership in Taiwan. The South Korean government denied its plans to shift recognition until the last moment, even when directly questioned by Taipei, informing Taiwan officials just three days before it planned to close Taipei's embassy in Seoul.[12] This abrupt shift in ties led to deep resentment, magnified by the fact that South Korea was the only remaining Asian nation to recognize Taiwan.[13] Since this time, South Korea has maintained a One China policy.

Today, relations between the two nations are largely economic and cultural. The Korean Mission in Taipei functions as the representative for the ROK government in Taiwan, with its counterpart the Taipei Mission in Korea in Seoul. It serves as the primary diplomatic body between the two entities and, unlike other countries' unofficial diplomatic representation in Taipei, the mission falls directly under the control of the Korean Ministry of Foreign Affairs. Direct ties between South Korea and Taiwan are most significant in the economic realm. In 2020, Taiwan ranked sixth in terms of both South Korean imports and exports.[14] Interviewees noted that Taiwan and the ROK also share relations in cultural arenas, including sister-

---

[10] Hong Liu, "The Sino-South Korean Normalization: A Triangular Explanation," *Asian Survey*, Vol. 33, No. 11, November 1, 1993.

[11] Liu, 1993.

[12] Lee, 2022b.

[13] Parris H. Chang, "The Taiwan-PRC Competition on the Korean Peninsula," *Korean Journal of Defense Analysis*, Vol. 13, No. 1, 2001.

[14] For the purposes of these data, we treat trade with Hong Kong separate from that of mainland China (Observatory of Economic Complexity, "South Korea Exports Data," undated-b).

city programs and educational exchange.[15] Further, interviewees described that there was an affinity between the people of South Korea and Taiwan as Western-style democratic nations.[16] Finally, interviewees said that the ROK and Taiwan engage in military exchange programs, but we were unable to find any publicly available documentation of such programs in English.

Relations with China and the United States: Revolves Around North Korea

The ROK seeks to maintain positive ties with both the United States and China as part of its strategy to manage the threat from North Korea. Seoul looks to Washington for security assistance and to Beijing to possibly help in reining in Pyongyang.[17]

China

The Yoon Suk-yeol administration is seeking positive ties with China. The administration's 2022 *Strategy for a Free, Peaceful, and Prosperous Indo-Pacific Region* describes China as "a key partner for achieving prosperity and peace in the Indo-Pacific region" and notes that the two nations will "pursue shared interests based on mutual respect and reciprocity."[18] Notably, China is not considered the ROK's main security challenge. Instead, the military threat posed by North Korea, officially called the Democratic People's Republic of Korea (DPRK), dominates South Korean security con-

---

[15] For example, it was noted in our interviews that the cultural impact of K-Pop in Taiwan was significant.

[16] One interviewee suggested that the same was not true of Japan.

[17] There is some difference in emphasis across the political spectrum: Conservatives historically stress the importance of the alliance with the United States more than progressives, who place greater weight on the importance of positive relations with China. Still, in broad terms, all South Korean leaders value the alliance with the United States and seek to achieve good relations with China.

[18] Republic of Korea, *Strategy for a Free, Peaceful, and Prosperous Indo-Pacific Region*, 2022, p. 14.

cerns.[19] The relationship between South Korea and China must therefore be viewed through the lens of North Korea and its relationship with the PRC. South Korea seeks positive relations with China due to its perceived ability to moderate DPRK behavior.[20] As a case in point, former President Moon Jae-in, a progressive, stated in 2021 that South Korea needs "the constructive efforts of China to enable denuclearization of DPRK."[21] After meeting with PRC President Xi Jinping, current ROK President Yoon Suk-yeol, a conservative, also called for China to play a greater role in reining in DPRK nuclear tests and other provocations.[22]

A desire to maintain good relations with China is reflected in how Seoul approaches sensitive issues, such as Taiwan. Several interviewees expressed fear that in a conflict over Taiwan, the PRC may encourage the DPRK to take direct military action against the ROK, given that it could help distract U.S. forces. Interviewees therefore noted reluctance within the ROK to make statements or take actions regarding Taiwan that may threaten its relationship with China.

Moreover, the ROK does not discuss the security challenges posed by China in official statements and documents, as the governments of Japan and the Philippines do. This is not only due the DPRK issue. Our interviews suggest that, at least in the near term, South Korean elites genuinely do not view the PRC as a direct military threat. Tensions have occasionally arisen over PRC incursions in South Korea's Exclusive Economic Zone,

---

[19] We do not focus on South Korean perceptions of threat from DPRK here. See, for example, Gian Gentile, Yvonne K. Crane, Dan Madden, Timothy M. Bonds, Bruce W. Bennett, Michael J. Mazarr, and Andrew Scobell, *Four Problems on the Korean Peninsula: North Korea's Expanding Nuclear Capabilities Drive a Complex Set of Problems*, RAND Corporation, TL-271-A, 2019.

[20] However, scholars have noted that even at a high point for ROK-PRC relations, China has been reluctant—and perhaps unable—to exert significant pressure on DPRK (Ji-Young Lee, *The Geopolitics of South Korea–China Relations: Implications for U.S. Policy in the Indo-Pacific*, RAND Corporation, PE-A524-1, 2020).

[21] Mark E. Manyin, Caitlin Campbell, Emma Chanlett-Avery, Mary Beth D. Nikitin, and Brock R. Williams, *U.S.–South Korea Relations*, Congressional Research Service, R41481, updated February 24, 2022, p. 45.

[22] Hyonhee Shin, "South Korea Urges Bigger China Role in Curbing North Korean Arms Tests," Reuters, November 15, 2022b.

and the two states have an ongoing territorial dispute over Socotra Rock.[23] However, these disputes are not as contentious as those between China and Japan or China and the Philippines. South Korean officials have noted their dedication to a rules-based order, democratic values, protection of human rights, and a free, peaceful, and prosperous Indo-Pacific region.[24] At the same time, ROK officials have been reluctant to call out China for behavior that runs counter to these goals.[25]

Still, there remain long-term concerns about China's potential challenge as a major military power, even if these concerns are not expressed publicly. In our interviews, South Korean respondents noted concerns about China's growing military capabilities and expressed their belief that an authoritarian, PRC-led order would neither be free nor rules-based and would ultimately be bad for both South Korean military and economic security. As one respondent noted, the ROK "thinks China is a systemic challenge to the region."

The more immediate potential danger posed by China to the ROK is in the economic realm, a view that was voiced unanimously among all respondents. The economic relationship between the ROK and China is quite complex. China is a major economic partner for South Korea but has leveraged economic ties coercively to oppose South Korean policies. ROK economic reliance on China remains very high, a fact that was consistently noted by our interviewees. In 2020, 24.7 percent of South Korean exports went to China, and 24.6 percent of South Korean imports came from China, making China South Korea's largest trade partner by some margin, and more recent data suggest that this has not changed.[26] By comparison, trade with the United States accounts for 14.1 percent of South Korea's exports and 12 percent of its imports.[27] Because of this reliance, one respondent noted that the

---

[23] Young Kil Park, "The Role of Fishing Disputes in China–South Korea Relations," Maritimes Awareness Project, April 23, 2020b.

[24] "United States–Republic of Korea Leaders' Joint Statement," May 21, 2022; Republic of Korea, *Strategy for a Free, Peaceful, and Prosperous Indo-Pacific Region*, 2022.

[25] Soo Kim, "Takeaways from the Biden-Moon Summit: Three Observations on China," *RAND Blog*, June 7, 2021.

[26] Observatory of Economic Complexity, undated-b.

[27] Observatory of Economic Complexity, undated-b.

ROK's economic interests "cause hesitation" with reorienting policies that touch on Chinese interests.

Interviewees noted that China's current ability to wield economic power coercively is a major concern and a significant factor in ROK reluctance to take a position in opposition to China, such as on Taiwan.[28] Our interviews consistently highlighted China's use of economic coercion against the ROK when the United States deployed a Terminal High-Altitude Area Defense (THAAD) battery in South Korea in 2016. While both the ROK and the United States specifically identified the THAAD battery as a defensive measure against North Korean missiles, China argued that the THAAD's radars could be used to spy on China.[29] China responded with a number of economically damaging, unofficial sanctions.[30] The PRC cut tourism to South Korea in half, resulting in nearly $7 billion in revenue according to the ROK National Assembly Budget.[31] Other industries suffered considerable declines: Food exports from the ROK to China dropped more than 5 percent from the prior year, and Korean auto sales in China dropped more than 50 percent.[32] The total economic impact was substantial: South Korea's yearly trade volume dropped from $227.3 billion to $211.4 billion in the midst of the crisis.[33] According to one respondent, these actions caused South Koreans to "suffer a lot."

---

[28] Negative public opinion toward China is also driven by concerns about economic coercion. Michael Lee, "Koreans Are Growing Much Less Fond of China," *Korea Joong-Ang Daily*, August 22, 2022a.

[29] For a summary of this case, see Michael J. Mazarr et al., *Understanding Influence in the Strategic Competition with China*, RAND Corporation, RR-A290-1, 2021.

[30] China denies that these measures were retaliation for the THAAD deployment.

[31] Ethan Meick and Nargiza Salidjanova, *China's Response to U.S.–South Korean Missile Defense System Deployment and Its Implications*, U.S.-China Economic and Security Review Commission, 2017, pp. 7-8; Matt Stiles, "Upset over a U.S. Missile Defense System, China Hits South Korea Where It Hurts—in the wallet," *Los Angeles Times*, February 28, 2018.

[32] "Korea's Food Exports to China Slide in March over THAAD Row," *Korea Herald*, April 4, 2017; Meick and Salidjanova, 2017, pp. 7-8.

[33] Bo-gyung Kim, "South Korea-China Trade Volume Rises to Pre-THAAD Levels," *Korea Herald*, December 19, 2018.

While the ROK did not reverse its decision, it did make a number of verbal assurances known collectively as the Three No's to reduce tensions: no additional deployment of THAAD batteries, no participation in the U.S. missile defense network, and no joining of a trilateral alliance with the United States and Japan. Since then, the Yoon administration has reopened the debate over its commitment to these assurances.[34] Still, as one interviewee noted, the THAAD episode has left a lasting mark on Korean thinking, saying that the possibility of Chinese retaliation "gets into our head" when discussing China-related policies, including anything that touches on Taiwan.

United States

Despite a desire to maintain positive relations with China, the United States remains the predominant security partner for South Korea, including the permanent presence of significant forces and military capabilities in the ROK. All respondents noted the importance the ROK places on the United States for its security. While the growing geopolitical competition between the United States and China is a cause for concern, or as one respondent said, makes the ROK "uneasy," the ROK understands the United States is committed to the ROK's security. That said, several respondents questioned Washington's ability to remain committed at the same levels it has in the past. One respondent noted that "the U.S. of today is not the U.S. of the Cold War, it is not the hegemon today like before," which constrains the capabilities it can commit to the region.

The current relationship between the governments of South Korea and the United States is, by all accounts, very strong, with the Yoon administration said to be placing a priority on the ROK's alliance with the United States. This is evident in a joint statement between Biden and Yoon in May 2022, where both leaders referred to the alliance as the linchpin for peace and

---

[34] Kang Seung-woo, "Seoul Reiterates that '3 Nos' Policy Is Not Commitment to China," *Korea Times*, August 10, 2022; Hyonhee Shin, "South Korea, China Clash over U.S. Missile Shield, Complicating Conciliation," Reuters, August 11, 2022a.

prosperity in the region.[35] The statement referred to the alliance as a global comprehensive strategic alliance "advancing freedom, peace, and prosperity in the Indo-Pacific region and beyond."[36] In early 2023, the Republic of Korea released the *Strategy for a Free, Peaceful, and Prosperous Indo-Pacific Region*, which highlighted the government's intent to further strengthen the alliance with the United States based on their shared commitment to the values of freedom, democracy, human rights, and the rule of law.[37]

View of Taiwan: Not a Direct Priority

Taiwan has not historically been considered a primary security concern in South Korea. According to one interviewee, the ROK does not pay much attention to it because "it's not [our] business." However, the ROK's relationship with the United States and increased tensions in the Taiwan Strait have made the issue more prominent in recent years. But balancing this relationship with the need to avoid antagonizing China puts the ROK in a "serious policy dilemma" over Taiwan, making any discussion of Taiwan a very sensitive topic, a point reiterated by every interviewee.

Although South Korea still seeks to avoid provoking China, it is now openly addressing the importance of the Taiwan Strait in ways it did not previously. Our interviews suggest that this is because U.S. policy on Taiwan is extremely important for ROK policy on Taiwan. As one interviewee characterized it, U.S. policy is a guideline for the ROK that stipulates the parameters, but "it is not the word of God." This provides the ROK latitude on its policies, reflected, for example, in the time it took for Seoul and Taipei to normalize ties. Still, this means that movement in U.S. policies does influence thinking in the ROK. And there was a consensus among respondents that recent moves by the Biden administration have caused policymakers in Seoul to discuss the Taiwan issue for the first time. This was evident in the

---

[35] "United States–Republic of Korea Leaders' Joint Statement," 2022. Similar statements were made under the previous ROK regime ("U.S.-ROK Leaders' Joint Statement," 2021.)

[36] "United States–Republic of Korea Leaders' Joint Statement," 2022.

[37] Republic of Korea, 2022, pp. 13–14.

2021 U.S.-ROK joint statement, marking the first time for the presidents of both countries to explicitly reference the importance of preserving "peace and stability in the Taiwan Strait."[38] This phrase, which is consistent with official PRC policy of peaceful reunification, was carefully chosen to avoid language that may provoke China.[39] Still, mention of the Taiwan issue was a notable change, as Moon represented the Democratic Party of Korea, which had historically maintained stronger ties with China. Our interviews made it clear that this shift to align policy with the United States was made in large part to gain a U.S. commitment for South Korea's main security priority: U.S. support of Moon's efforts to restart dialogue with the North.[40]

This shift has endured a turnover in ROK government. Most recently, the Yoon administration's *Strategy for a Free, Peaceful, and Prosperous Indo-Pacific Region* notes "the importance of peace and stability in the Taiwan Strait for the peace and stability of the Korean Peninsula and for the security and prosperity of the Indo-Pacific."[41] Our interviews revealed several ways in which Taiwan, while not a direct security priority, may be an issue that affects the ROK.

Our interviews suggest that the ROK is concerned about how U.S. involvement in a war over Taiwan might affect the ROK, with a unanimous concern that it would be the ROK to be the first to suffer from coercion if the United States takes actions that push back against China. This was based on the belief that should a military contingency occur, North Korea will use the opportunity to attack U.S. forces in South Korea—either with or without the direct support of China. There is also a fear that the United States would prioritize the defense of Taiwan over that of South Korea in such an

---

[38] "U.S.-ROK Leaders' Joint Statement," 2021. A 2022 statement between President Biden and President Yoon used stronger language, stating that preserving peace and stability in the Taiwan Strait is an "essential element in security and prosperity in the Indo-Pacific region" (United States–Republic of Korea Leaders' Joint Statement, 2022).

[39] "S. Korea Has Refrained from Comments on China's Internal Affairs: FM," Yonhap News Agency, May 25, 2021.

[40] For a discussion of the result of these trades, see also Rafiq Dossani, "The Biden-Moon Meetings: Much Ado About Something?" *RAND Blog*, June 4, 2021.

[41] Republic of Korea, 2022, pp. 13–14.

event, including moving assets from the peninsula to engage in the fight over Taiwan.

Interviewees were also concerned that the United States would seek to employ forces based in South Korea to defend Taiwan (e.g., staging forces, providing rear support, or even launching combat sorties). Consequently, respondents worried that U.S. use of its bases in South Korea could make the country a PRC target. Some interviewees expressed concern that China might target these U.S. forces early in a conflict to prevent their use for the defense of Taiwan, which would also make defending the ROK from a possible DPRK attack more difficult. These entanglement concerns were more significant than fears that the United States may abandon its commitment to the ROK.

In addition, our discussions revealed that concerns over Taiwan's security were not purely motivated by the ROK relationship with the United States. Reflecting on the THAAD experience, interviewees noted with concern that any conflict over Taiwan would potentially be damaging economically for the ROK, not simply because China and Taiwan are both significant trading partners, as is the United States, but because so much of ROK commerce travels through the Strait.[42] Further, in the event that the PRC forcefully reunifies Taiwan with the mainland, China would maintain greater control over the sea lines of communication that are so vital for ROK trade. As a result, interviewees worried China would possess even greater economic leverage over South Korea.

Respondents were concerned about stability in the Taiwan Strait, but they argued that recent U.S. diplomacy has been unnecessarily provocative without enhancing deterrence. For example, the visit by Speaker Pelosi was not well received. In significant part, this was due to the timing of the visit.[43] By visiting Taiwan directly before the Chinese Communist Party's National Congress, interviewees believed, Pelosi put significant pressure on Xi Jinping to respond in some fashion and provided the pretext for increased Chinese military activities around Taiwan. Yoon did not meet with her during

---

[42] As of late 2022, the United States ranks second in terms of both South Korean imports and exports.

[43] Some suggested that official visits were, in general, likely to receive little attention by the ROK government.

her trip, and interviewees believe this was because he did not want to associate himself with policy statements about Taiwan she might make.[44]

Often, respondents noted, it is the public nature of U.S. statements that is most concerning, particularly when they appear provocative and approach China's redlines. For instance, interviewees believed China already understood the extent of the U.S. commitment to Taiwan prior to Biden's comments. One respondent noted that his remarks were "burdensome when the ROK has been so careful." Another noted that actions such as these are provocative and could provoke China to lash out at U.S. allies or could lead North Korea to take action against South Korea. A third respondent summarized these concerns as making the United States "look like a revisionist power." There was a strong sense among respondents that U.S. policy should do a better job of striking a balance between provocation and deterrence. Maintaining the status quo is therefore strongly preferred.

ROK Views of Hypothetical Changes in U.S. Taiwan Policy

South Korean perceptions on any hypothetical change in U.S. Taiwan policy hinged on what any change would mean for regional stability and therefore for the ROK. Specifically, as already noted, interviewees argued the United States should strike a balance between deterrence and provocation. While interviewees noted that the ROK wants to be a good ally and support the United States, they are also concerned about potential Chinese responses against the ROK for supporting the United States. When actions are taken, the ROK does not want the United States to push back too hard or too little on PRC behavior, but rather push back in a proportional way. If the PRC takes aggressive action, the United States should push back; but if the PRC were to take a more cooperative stance, the United States ought to do the same.

As with interviewees in Japan and, as we will discuss in Chapter 5, the Philippines, certain hypothetical U.S. policy changes proved entirely

---

[44] Others noted a second explanation: that her visit simply coincided with an already planned vacation by President Yoon.

uncontroversial among interviewees in South Korea. Enhanced economic cooperation, for example, was seen as a benefit to all parties. Because South Korea and Taiwan are already significant trading partners, there was broad support for increasing the integration of Taiwan into the regional economic institutions, such as the CPTPP, and for further bilateral economic ties between Taiwan and both South Korea and the United States. That said, there was an opinion that these stronger economic ties should not require Taiwan statehood or come at the expense of isolating China. And in the diplomatic space, interviewees broadly supported the idea of Taiwan being included in diplomatic bodies that did not require statehood, such as the World Health Assembly, especially given the region's experience with the coronavirus disease 2019 pandemic. However, respondents noted that this would need to be done in a balanced manner so as not to provoke China.

There was also no pushback on increased intelligence sharing. Respondents believed that it was already understood that the United States and Taiwan shared intelligence. Further, respondents believed that continued intelligence sharing was important not just in the event of a possible conflict, but also to reduce the possibility that escalation could occur unintentionally.

South Korean interviewees prefer status quo U.S. diplomatic polices and oppose changes that signal an increased or decreased U.S. commitment to Taiwan. Because of their perceived effect on maintaining regional stability, respondents generally favored the United States continuing to issue diplomatic statements about it not being worth the cost for China to use force against Taiwan, and joint diplomatic statements with other like-minded states calling for stability in the Taiwan Strait.

Respondents were reluctant to support statements that appear to veer from inclusiveness and explicitly meant to "deter China" or "help Taiwan." Moreover, interviewees believed that increasing high-level visits would be provocative and preferred to return to the status quo prior to the Pelosi visit, noting that the PRC actively opposes even low-level official visits between Taiwan and the ROK. Likewise, interviewees argued that official statements further resolving strategic ambiguity in favor of a clear commitment to Taiwan would likely provoke China and do little to change the ability of the United States to deter malign Chinese actions. One group of analysts argued that if the United States were to continue making gestures, it would need to ensure corresponding military policies to deter China from responding too aggressively. Either way, analysts agreed the ROK would not follow the U.S. lead in these areas of increasing diplomatic support to Taiwan. While Seoul would be unlikely to push back against U.S. behavior, such diplomatic statements would cause concern within the ROK government because of the expectation that this would cross a red line for China.

At the same time, interviewees in the ROK did not want the United States to reduce its commitment to Taiwan, either. Some respondents viewed such reductions as signaling U.S. "weakness," a "U.S. retreat from the region," or "a weakening of U.S. credibility." Simply stated by one interviewee, such actions send the "wrong message" to China. Respondents frequently favored strategic ambiguity. Statements like those made by Biden were seen as deviating from the norm. Rather than expressing a reduced commitment to Taiwan, respondents favored returning to that baseline.

Interviewees disagreed over the value of the United States increasing military support to Taiwan. Many interviewees saw arms sales and military training for Taiwan as bilateral issues between the United States and Taiwan in which the ROK had no stake and would offer no opinion. Others supported improvements in Taiwan's military capabilities, especially to keep up with PRC military modernization. Further, while some respondents noted that increased arms sales may provoke a Chinese response, many believed that PRC responses to the arms sales were already normalized.

On the issue of arms transfers, there also existed two minority sentiments that were seemingly at odds with one another. The first suggested that increases in arms sales might embolden Taiwan to take greater steps toward independence. Another interviewee argued that increasing arms sales to Taiwan would signal that the United States would not be willing to intervene directly in a Taiwan Strait conflict. Although offered by different groups, each thought increasing U.S. arms sales to Taiwan might make conflict more likely.

There was greater consensus among respondents on issues relating to U.S. military presence. Interviewees expected that increasing U.S. presence in the region would increase the U.S. ability to deter the DPRK, in addition to China. Respondents, therefore, supported this initiative because they saw it as a way to deter China from attacking Taiwan without being overly provocative. However, there was significant nuance expressed in response to this question. Several respondents said that, if these forces were placed in the ROK, this would raise concern about what the United States would ask the ROK to contribute in the event of a conflict. One respondent expressed concerns about PRC economic pressure if these forces were placed on the peninsula. Further, respondents expressed concern that increases in U.S. regional presence might be insufficient or would be indicative that a conflict over Taiwan was already impending.

Increasing the U.S. military presence in and around Taiwan, however, including increased freedom of navigation operations and an increased footprint on the island, was seen as more provocative. Some interviewees did not want the United States to engage in such actions, which have the potential to provoke a militarized response and unintended escalation, though a minority said that this would be a positive signal of U.S. commitment to the region.

At the same time, South Korean interviewees did not want to see a more distant military relationship between the United States and Taiwan. These experts and policymakers were concerned that any reduction in support to Taiwan may be indicative of a lower commitment to the region more broadly and the ROK specifically, despite the existence of a mutual defense treaty with the United States. There were also more proximate concerns about what these activities would mean for the ROK. For example, a reduction of U.S. freedom of navigation operations through the Taiwan Strait might embolden China to take actions that endanger ROK maritime commerce.

A reduction of U.S. forces in the region, while not considered especially likely, would be considered especially alarming (particularly if it meant a reduction from the Korean Peninsula).[45] Interviewees believed this policy would harm ROK security by weakening deterrence against DPRK aggression. A reduction in U.S. forces would not only reduce U.S. military capability to respond to DPRK attacks but would also be seen as a clear signal of declining U.S. interests in the region. One respondent went as far as saying it would spark fears of a "power vacuum of U.S. withdrawal." This would in turn lead to worry that the United States does not place a high value on the Korean Peninsula and may not be willing to fulfill its commitments to

---

[45] For the same reason, an increase in the regional U.S. presence was broadly supported, though there remained statements of concern about what PRC and DPRK responses might entail.

South Korean defense. That is, while interviewees expressed greater concern about entanglement than abandonment today, reductions in U.S. presence could make them fear abandonment to a greater extent.

In such an instance, interviewees were not certain how Seoul would respond. Under the current administration, they believed that the ROK would seek to maintain closer ties with the United States and persuade the United States to recommit to security in the Indo-Pacific. This was in line with descriptions of the importance that the ROK government places on the alliance, particularly in light of the DPRK threat. Interviewees also noted that Seoul could choose additional measures to improve its security position. This included taking steps to provide more for its own defense, including the development of nuclear weapons, an idea currently making headlines in light of North Korean aggression.[46] Respondents suggested that Seoul may also seek greater cooperation with other regional states.

There was sentiment that future governments, particularly progressive governments, which have sought a stronger relationship with China in the past, may seek closer ties with China if fears about U.S. abandonment become significant. Respondents noted that Seoul already takes key demands from Beijing very seriously and made it clear that the ROK would not be able to stand up to pressure from China alone, if the U.S. presence waned. However, respondents noted that even progressive governments do not believe that China's influence on the DPRK alone can provide for the defense of the ROK. As a result, the ROK would have strong incentives to first try to draw the United States closer to maintain its support against the DPRK. Therefore, while drawing closer to China would be a possibility, Seoul would have to be extremely fearful of abandonment by the United States to truly turn away from its alliance and toward closer ties with China.

Conclusion

South Korean sentiment on U.S.-Taiwan cooperation is full of tensions. ROK respondents saw the United States signaling commitment to Taiwan

---

[46] Choe Sang-Hun, "In a First, South Korea Declares Nuclear Weapons a Policy Option," *New York Times*, January 12, 2023.

was a good sign for U.S. commitment to the ROK but also feared that U.S. actions toward Taiwan could lead to a conflict that threatens ROK security. Similarly, interviewees want the United States to push back on China to enhance regional deterrence, but fear that pushing back too strongly could provoke China to use military force.

These competing considerations affect how the ROK views potential changes in U.S. policy.

Interviewees did not have concerns about increasing U.S. intelligence and economic ties with Taiwan, because these policies were not thought to elicit a strong response from China. However, interviewees opposed increases in U.S. diplomatic support to Taiwan, such as an explicit security guarantee or more high-level visits, which were seen as, on net, destabilizing. Respondents said that some military steps like increased arms sales would be stabilizing, while others said that such increased military activities near Taiwan or training activities in Taiwan would be destabilizing. Ultimately, our interviews suggest that South Korea largely prefers status quo U.S. policies toward Taiwan (Tables 4.1 and 4.2).

TABLE 4.1

The ROK's Perspective on U.S. Options for Increasing Support to Taiwan

	U.S. Policy Option	The ROK's Perspective
Diplomatic	Advocate for Taiwan's inclusion in fora that do not require statehood	Mixed feelings
	Increase warnings directed at China about the costs of attacking Taiwan	Mixed feelings
	Increase emphasis on Taiwan in joint statements	Mixed feelings
	Increase high-level official interactions	Does not support
	Explicitly state that the United States will defend Taiwan	Does not support
Military	Increase regional presence	Mixed feelings
	Increase arms sales and security assistance to Taiwan	Mixed feelings
	Increase U.S. presence in or near Taiwan	Mixed feelings
	Pursue a bilateral free trade agreement	Support
	Support Taiwan's inclusion in regional trade agreements	Support
	Increased intelligence sharing	Neutral

NOTE: Interviewees expected the government to support increases in regional presence, but disagreed on how the government would weigh China's response to increases in the ROK itself.

TABLE 4.2

The ROK's Perspective on U.S. Options for Decreasing Support to Taiwan

	U.S. Policy Option	The ROK's Perspective
Diplomatic	Decrease high-level official interactions (e.g., Cabinet or senior congressional leaders)	Mixed feelings
	Decrease warnings to China about the costs of attacking Taiwan	Does not support
	Decrease emphasis on Taiwan in joint statements	Does not support
	Explicitly state that the United States will not defend Taiwan	Does not support
Military	Decrease regional presence	Does not support
	Decrease arms sales and security assistance	Does not support
	Decrease U.S. presence in or near Taiwan	Does not support
Economic and information	Reduce economic ties	Does not support
	Increased intelligence sharing	Neutral

CHAPTER 5

The Philippines

Ties between the Philippines and Taiwan have been consistent even as Manila's ties with China and the United States have shifted. Manila's number one priority issue with Taipei remains the presence of over 150,000 Philippine citizens working in Taiwan—which are referred to officially as *Overseas Filipino Workers*—and the remittances they send. Beyond these economic ties, the security dimensions of the Taiwan Strait remain under-developed in Philippine strategic thinking. However, one thing is clear: The Philippines seeks to avoid provoking China on issues sensitive to Beijing. Understanding that the Philippines has much to lose should a regional conflict break out over Taiwan, Philippine officials prefer maintenance of the status quo on all issues relating to Taiwan.

History of the Philippines' Relations with Taiwan

Following its independence from Japan, Manila established its Philippine Legation in Nanjing, China, in 1946, with several consulates opening in subsequent years. In 1949, however, the Philippines closed all diplomatic posts in mainland China and, following Washington's lead, opened an embassy in Taipei on March 1, 1956.[1] Manila's relations with Beijing were hostile in the decades that followed, as the threat of Chinese aid to the New People's Army, an armed Communist group in the Philippines, was an ever-present

---

[1] Philippine Consulate General in Xiamen China, "About Us: Historical Background," webpage, undated.

concern.[2] Following the U.S. rapprochement with the PRC, Manila moved in a similar fashion. On May 11, 1972, President Ferdinand E. Marcos opened trade relations with the PRC and other socialist countries.[3] With many countries beginning to establish formal diplomatic ties with the PRC, the Philippines initially espoused a "Two China" policy at the United Nations (UN), in which both the PRC and Taiwan would be represented.[4] After the UN recognized the PRC as the government of China and ejected Taiwan as a member, Manila formally established diplomatic ties with Beijing on June 9, 1975.[5] Manila adopted a "One China" policy in a joint communiqué, which stated, "The Philippine Government recognizes the Government of the [PRC] as the sole legal government of China, fully understands and respects the position of the Chinese Government that there is but one China and that Taiwan is an integral part of Chinese territory."[6]

Recognition of Beijing meant that the Philippine embassy in Taiwan was closed. In its place, Manila established unofficial relations through a nonprofit organization that could act as the Philippine representative office in Taiwan, today called the Manila Economic and Cultural Office.[7] Over the years, the Philippines has limited its relationship with Taiwan through a series of presidential actions prohibiting governmental visits to Taiwan and meetings with Taiwanese officials.[8]

---

2 Library of Congress, Federal Research Division, "Country Studies: Relations with Asian Neighbors," webpage, undated. The New People's Army was the armed wing of the Communist Party of the Philippines.

3 Philippine Consulate General in Xiamen China, undated.

4 National Defense College of the Philippines, "Philippine Foreign Policy and the Complexities of Cross-Strait Relations," February 6, 2023.

5 Philippine Consulate General in Xiamen China, undated.

6 Joint Communiqué of the Government of the People's Republic of China and the Government of the Republic of the Philippines, June 9, 1975.

7 The original organization was called the Far East Trade Promotion Center, which later became the Asian Exchange Center, Inc. On January 1, 1993, Manila changed the name to the Manila Economic and Cultural Office (Philippine Representative Office in Taiwan, Manila Economic and Cultural Office, "Who We Are," webpage, undated).

8 These were President of the Philippines, Executive Order 313, "Prohibiting Philippine Government Officials to Visit Taiwan or to Receive Calls by Visiting Taiwanese Officials," signed December 17, 1987; and Republic of the Philippines, Presidential

As it does in other countries, Taiwan has a counterpart organization called the Taipei Economic and Cultural Office in the Philippines. Through these offices, the two have "maintained close relations in the areas of economy, trade, law enforcement, labor affairs, tourism, education, and culture."[9] Beyond these ties, the two sides regularly engage in sister-city relationships, engagement and collaboration by university alliances, and exchanges between religious and humanitarian organizations.[10]

Relations with China and the United States: Balancing Between Countries

The Philippines seeks to balance its relationship with the United States and China due to its reliance on the former for security and the latter for economics. Individual Philippine leaders have had different instincts about how to strike this balance. However, Philippine leaders have reacted similarly, by drawing closer to the United States when faced with more assertive Chinese behavior.

China

The Philippines faces countervailing pressures in its bilateral relationship with China. On one hand, the Philippines relies heavily on China economically. China is the Philippines' largest trading partner, export destination, and source of imports.[11] In 2020, for example, 16.2 percent of Philippine exports went to China (compared with 13.5 percent to the United States)

Memorandum Circular No. 148, "Prescribing the Guidelines for the Implementation of Executive Order No. 313," 1987; information from National Defense College of the Philippines, "Philippine Foreign Policy and the Complexities of Cross-Strait Relations," February 6, 2023.

[9] Ministry of Foreign Affairs (Republic of China), "ROC Congratulates Philippines on Conclusion of Its General Elections," May 12, 2016.

[10] Brian Doce, "People-Centric Diplomacy and Philippine-Taiwan Relations," *Facts Asia*, November 30, 2021.

[11] Jason Hung, "China's Soft Power Grows in the Philippines," *The Diplomat*, February 26, 2021.

and 31.9 percent of its imports come from China (compared with 6.31 percent from the United States).[12] On the other hand, the Philippines has active territorial disputes with China.[13] This creates incentives for the Philippines to turn toward the United States, its key security partner.

Upon coming to office, President Rodrigo Duterte reversed his predecessor's policies by prioritizing improved relations with China. A deterioration of bilateral ties with the United States over human rights issues and a charm offensive by China reinforced this policy, leading to Duterte's September 2016 decision to "open alliances" with China (and Russia).[14] The following month, he declared his military and economic "separation" from the United States and that he had "realigned" himself with China, becoming dependent on China "for all times."[15] China subsequently made economic pledges worth $24 billion and relaxed non-tariff barriers on Philippine fruit exports.[16] Reflecting his more conciliatory approach to China, Duterte avoided discussion of territorial disputes.[17] Then, in 2018, he announced his intention to seek joint oil and gas exploration with China in the South China Sea.

Despite China's public comments, its military activities against Philippine interests did not cease, serving to harden Manila's relationship with Beijing.[18] The 2017 National Security Policy describes territorial disputes

---

[12] OEC, "Philippines," webpage, accessed August 1, 2021.

[13] Maritime Awareness Project, *Philippines*, National Bureau of Asian Research, undated.

[14] Manuel Mogato, "Philippines' Duterte Wants to 'Open Alliances' with Russia, China," Reuters, September 26, 2016.

[15] Rodrigo Roa Duterte, "Speech During the Philippines-China Trade and Investment Forum," Speech, Beijing, China, October 20, 2016.

[16] This included $9 billion in soft loans and economic deals including $15 billion in investments (Andreo Calonzo and Cecilia Yap, "China Visit Helps Duterte Reap Funding Deals Worth $24 Billion," Bloomberg, October 21, 2016; Richard Javad Heydarian, "Duterte's Uncertain China Gamble," Asia Maritime Transparency Initiative, November 3, 2016.

[17] Manolo Serapio Jr. and Petty Martin, "Philippines' Duterte Says Pointless Discussing South China Sea Woes at Summit," Reuters, April 27, 2017.

[18] Derek Grossman, "China Has Lost the Philippines Despite Duterte's Best Efforts," *Foreign Policy*, May 3, 2021.

as the "foremost security challenge to Philippines' sovereignty and territorial integrity."[19] The 2018 National Defense Strategy goes one step further, naming China and calling out the construction of artificial islands "as a grave threat to [the Philippines] national security."[20] From roughly 2019 onward, Chinese maritime forces (i.e., maritime militia, China Coast Guard, People's Liberation Army Navy) increased their aggressive behavior against the Philippine Coast Guard and Armed Forces of the Philippines (AFP) in the South China Sea and near Philippine-claimed territory.[21] Because of this, Duterte slowly backed away from China. Rather than advocating greater cooperation with China, the Duterte administration began to file diplomatic warnings against China, call out Chinese behavior, and even threaten China with military action.[22] Duterte even told the UN General Assembly in 2020 that his government "firmly reject[ed] attempts to undermine" the issue of Philippines disputes with China in the South China Sea.[23]

This sentiment appears to be largely unchanged with the Philippines' current president, Ferdinand Marcos Jr. Shortly after becoming president, Marcos emphasized diplomatic engagement. At the same time, he has expressed his strong support for Manila's 2016 court victory at the Hague, in reference to the Philippines' case against China under the UN Convention on the Law of the Sea to challenge China's nine-dash line claim.[24] He has

---

[19] Rodrigo Roa Duterte, "National Security Policy for Change and Well-Being of the Filipino People," Philippine Department of National Defense, April 1, 2017, p. 13.

[20] Department of Foreign Affairs (Republic of the Philippines), *National Defense Strategy 2018–2022*, November 1, 2018, p. 11.

[21] For a good summary of these events, please view Philippines-related articles by Richard Javad Heydarian, "Foreign Policy Under Marcos Jr.: More Like Father Than Outgoing Duterte," Asia Maritime Transparency Initiative, June 13, 2022.

[22] "Philippines' Duterte Would Send Navy Ships in South China Sea to Assert Claim over Resources," Reuters, April 19, 2021.

[23] Duterte, Rodrigo Roa, "Full Text: President Duterte's Speech at the 75th UN General Assembly," Rappler.com, September 23, 2020b.

[24] Sofia Tomacruz, "In Turnaround, Marcos Pledges to Uphold Hague Ruling," Rappler.com, May 26, 2022.

used this victory to argue for a stronger stance on South China Sea issues.[25] In a direct challenge to China, for example, Marcos has said "We have no conflicting claims with China. What we have is China making claims on our territory."[26] He has also stated that the Philippines "will not lose one inch of its territory."[27] While Marcos has sought to engage China and seek economic cooperation, he has not shied away from highlighting the security challenges posed by China. In doing so, Marcos appears to have adopted a "calibrated assertiveness towards China while welcoming pragmatic cooperation on the economic front."[28]

United States

The United States and the Philippines have maintained a formal treaty alliance since 1951, under which Washington pledges to defend the Philippines. Despite this alliance, bilateral relations are not always smooth, nor are the allies always in alignment. For example, throughout the Cold War, the two shared many strategic and economic interests and deep people-to-people ties, but the heavy dependence on the U.S. military left many in the Philippines with complicated views of bilateral ties. Rising anti-U.S. sentiment in the Philippines in the late 1980s and the changing threat environment at the end of the Cold War helped motivate both governments to engage in negotiations to determine the future of U.S. military presence. Despite signing a new treaty in 1991, the Philippine Senate rejected it, effectively terminating the Mutual Base Agreement and leading to the end of a permanent

[25] Bonnie S. Glaser and Charmaine Willoughby, "China's Relations with the Philippines Under Ferdinand "BongBong" Marcos, Jr.," *China Global Podcast*, 2022; Sebastian Strangio, "Philippines' Marcos to Pursue Bilateral Deal with Beijing Over South China Sea," *The Diplomat*, January 28, 2022b; Sebastian Strangio, "Philippines' Marcos Pledges to Uphold Landmark South China Sea Ruling," *The Diplomat*, May 27, 2022a.

[26] Jim Gomez, "Marcos Says Sea Feud Involving China Keeps Him up at Night," AP News, January 19, 2023.

[27] CNN Philippines Staff, "'PH Won't Lose an Inch of Its Territory,' says Marcos," CNN Philippines, February 18, 2023.

[28] Heydarian, 2022.

U.S. military presence.[29] Chinese forces' occupation of Mischief Reef in late 1994 prompted President Fidel Ramos to invite U.S. forces back in 1995 and negotiate a Visiting Forces Agreement (VFA).[30] And then, under President Benigno Aquino III, Manila signed a ten-year Enhanced Defense Cooperation Agreement (EDCA) in April 2014 allowing a rotational U.S. presence on AFP bases.

As noted above, when Duterte became president, he sought to change course in bilateral relations as part of his effort to "maintain an independent foreign policy."[31] Two actions in particular caused significant stress in the alliance. The first was his deliberate lean toward China and this "separation" from the United States. To demonstrate that separation, in September 2016 Duterte announced the alliance's Philippines Amphibious Landing Exercise scheduled for October 2016 would be the last military exercise with the United States during his six-year term (although it was later replaced by the Kamandag exercise).[32] Also in September, he announced that U.S. Special Forces in Mindanao must leave (although in 2017 Manila agreed to the U.S. Department of Defense launching Operation Pacific Eagle–Philippines to train the AFP to combat terrorism).[33] Finally, he refused to allow the United States to use the Philippines for U.S. Navy freedom of navigation

---

[29] Philip Shenon, "Philippine Senate Votes to Reject U.S. Base Renewal," *New York Times*, September 16, 1991; William Branigin, "U.S. Military Ends Role in Philippines," *Washington Post*, November 24, 1992; Andrew Yeo, *Activists, Alliances, and Anti-U.S. Base Protests*, Cambridge University Press, 2011.

[30] Thomas Lum and Ben Dolven, *The Republic of the Philippines and U.S. Interests—2014*, Congressional Research Service, May 15, 2014.

[31] Duterte, 2017, p. 25; Rodrigo Roa Duterte, "5th State of the Nation Address," Session Hall of the House of Representatives, July 27, 2020a.

[32] "US, Philippines Launch War Games Amid Uncertainty over Ties," *DW*, October 4, 2016; Seth Robson, "US-Filipino Troops Kick Off New Kamandag Exercise in the Philippines," *Stars and Stripes*, October 2, 2017.

[33] Of this amount, $267.75 million came from foreign military financing, $73 million in fiscal year 2018 assistance, another $278.8 million in U.S. Department of Defense security assistance, and over $8 million in international military education and training funds (Recto Mercene, "US Official: Military Aid to PHL Still Priority," *Business Monitor*, November 8, 2019).

operations.[34] His second action that caused significant stress in the alliance occurred in February 2020, when Duterte declared his intent to end the VFA, which would end the legal basis by which U.S. forces can train and exercise in the Philippines.

Despite this strain in the alliance, Manila maintained the alliance while espousing the strategic benefits it provides to the Philippines given ongoing Chinese provocations. For example, Duterte's 2017 National Security Policy says, "A continuing US security presence in the Asia Pacific is a stabilizing force. . . . The US remains as the sole defense treaty ally of the Philippines" and that the Mutual Defense Treaty "has been strengthened under the Enhanced Defense Cooperation Agreement (EDCA) of 2015."[35] His administration's 2018 National Defense Strategy similarly calls the United States a stabilizing presence in the region.[36] As Chinese provocations against the Philippines increased, those ties got stronger. In February 2021, Duterte publicly acknowledged the importance of the U.S. alliance by stating that the "exigency of the moment requires [the United States'] presence here."[37] Stemming from this, and following the expiration of the second suspension of the VFA termination process, in July 2021 Duterte decided to not abrogate the VFA.[38] In the weeks before leaving office, Duterte allowed the AFP to host one of the largest-ever iterations of the Balikatan military exercise.[39] And in November, the allies adopted the Joint Vision for a 21st Century Philippine–United States Partnership.

---

[34] Jim Gomez, "Philippines Says US On Its Own in South China Sea Patrols," *The Philippine Star,* December 8, 2016; Ryan Pickrell, "Firebrand Philippine President Pushes the US to Send the Entire 7th Fleet Into the South China Sea," *Business Insider,* July 8, 2019.

[35] Duterte, 2017, p. 89.

[36] Department of Foreign Affairs (Republic of the Philippines), 2018, p. 21.

[37] Renato Cruz de Castro, "Duterte Finally Admits the Importance of the U.S. Alliance," Asia Maritime Transparency Initiative, February 24, 2021.

[38] Duterte had previously suspended the termination process twice: June 2020, November 2020 ("Duterte Cancels Order to Terminate VFA with US," CNN Philippines, July 30, 2021).

[39] U.S. Embassy in the Philippines, "37th Iteration of Balikatan Exercise Set to Begin in the Philippines," March 22, 2022.

The election of Marcos suggests the Philippines will continue to emphasize relations with the United States as it seeks to balance those ties with China. For example, during his first meeting with President Biden, Marcos not only said "We have always considered the United States our partner, our ally, and our friend," but he acknowledged the important role the United States plays in maintaining regional peace.[40] Additionally, Marcos told Biden that the Philippines will "continue to look to the United States for . . . the maintenance of peace in our region" as partners, allies, and friends.[41] As one respondent noted, "We can't imagine a future without the U.S."

The Marcos administration's actions in early 2023 reinforced these statements. These policies included agreement to not only push for completion of projects at the existing five EDCA locations, but to designate four new locations in the Philippines for U.S. forces to have access.[42] The Philippines and the United States also agreed to resume joint patrols in the South China Sea.[43] These moves send an important signal to China that U.S.-Philippine security cooperation is moving closer together, with a cautious eye on Chinese actions in the region.

View of Taiwan: Not a Primary Concern Historically

Taiwan has never been a primary concern for Philippine foreign policy or a consideration in its relations with the United States or China. As one interviewee stated, "Taiwan doesn't figure into a lot of conversations" in the Philippines. And yet, some respondents noted that there is a genuine sympathy for Taiwan, given that the Philippines also bears the brunt of Chinese provocations. But there was a consensus that Taiwan largely figures into

---

[40] Rommel C. Banlaoi, "[Opinion] Flexible Foreign Policy: Balancing PH Relations with US, China Under Marcos Jr. Presidency," Rappler.com, October 19, 2022.

[41] Jim Gomez and Joeal Calupitan, "Marcos Jr. Reaffirms US Ties in First 100 Days of Presidency," AP News, October 7, 2022.

[42] U.S. Department of Defense, "Philippines, U.S. Announce Four New EDCA Sites," *DOD News*, February 1, 2023.

[43] "US, Philippines to Restart Joint Patrols in South China Sea," *Defense Post*, February 3, 2023.

Philippine thinking via economic ties.[44] In particular, Manila highly values the over 150,000 Philippine citizens working in Taiwan, which are referred to officially as Overseas Filipino Workers.[45] Beyond these workers, bilateral economic ties have grown in recent years. For example, Manila and Taipei signed a bilateral investment agreement, angering Beijing.[46] More recently, Philippine Foreign Secretary Enrique Manalo told visiting Secretary Antony J. Blinken that the Philippines would value greater economic cooperation with Taipei.[47] This view is reciprocated in Taipei, which views the Philippines as the gateway to the Association of Southeast Asian Nations in President Tsai Ing-wen's "New Southbound Policy."[48]

Yet, some respondents noted that there is a growing realization of the security aspects of Taiwan. For example, one respondent noted that the Philippines "is the most immediately affected country" if a war starts over Taiwan. It is for this reason that many Philippine security analysts have argued that the Philippines should see Taiwan's status and the risk of conflict in the Strait as a key Philippine concern for two reasons. First, if China were to succeed in invading Taiwan, it might be emboldened to use force to settle other territorial disputes, including those with the Philippines. Second, a war in the Taiwan Strait could harm the Philippine economy, both directly and indirectly through disruptions in financing, trade, and energy flows.[49]

---

[44] Asia Briefing, "Taiwan and the Philippines Work to Enhance Trade Ties," undated.

[45] Ministry of Foreign Affairs (Republic of China), "Taiwan-Philippines Relations," February 20, 2013.

[46] "China Unhappy as Philippines Signs Investment Deal with Taiwan," Reuters, December 8, 2017.

[47] U.S. Department of State, 2022.

[48] According to this policy, Taiwan hopes to strengthen cooperation with the Philippines in various fields, not only in trade and investment, agriculture, fisheries aquaculture, technology, small and medium enterprises, green technology, and climate change, but also in education, culture, and people-to-people interactions and exchanges (Ministry of Foreign Affairs [Republic of China]), 2013.

[49] Renato Cruz de Castro, "Can the Philippines Stay Neutral in a Taiwan Strait Military Confrontation Between the US and China?" *Think China*, October 5, 2022; Joshua Bernard Espeña, "A 'Taiwan Dilemma' for the Philippines," Atlas Institute for International Affairs, September 26, 2020; National Defense College of the Philippines, 2023.

Despite these arguments, the government has continued to focus primarily on the economic relationship with Taiwan, eschewing the security issues associated with the Taiwan Strait. For example, the 2018 Philippine National Defense Strategy downplayed the importance of cross-Strait tensions to Philippine security.[50] Instead, the document emphasized the potential for adverse economic effects, arguing that tensions among major powers over Taiwan "is a concern given their assistance to the country's development as well as Philippine economic and social interests in these countries as highlighted by the significance in trade and [overseas Filipino workers] deployed."[51] The fact that these workers' remittances are important to the Philippines economy is what matters most, leading some Philippine politicians to call for a contingency plan for evacuating them from Taiwan in case of conflict.[52]

Consistent with the Philippine desire to maintain stability in the Strait, when interviewees were asked about Biden's repeated comments on defending Taiwan, Pelosi's visit to Taiwan, and China's response to Pelosi's visit, interviewees described all as unhelpful "escalatory actions." One person even called the Biden and Pelosi actions as "taunting China." Yet, respondents were hesitant to explicitly label the United States or China as provocative even if their actions were a departure from the status quo.

Consistent with that view, Marcos has stated that his government is "certainly concerned about rising tensions in the Taiwan Strait," but instead of criticizing any country, he "urged all parties involved to exercise maximum restraint" and called for a peaceful resolution of issues involving Taiwan.[53] At the same time, he said he expected Manila's military ties with Washington would intensify given the increase in tensions.[54] The Philippine Depart-

---

[50] Department of Foreign Affairs (Republic of the Philippines), 2018, p. 13.

[51] Department of Foreign Affairs (Republic of the Philippines), 2018, p. 13.

[52] Paolo Romero, "Tulfo Seeks Contingency Plan for OFWs in Taiwan," *Philippine Star*, August 8, 2022.

[53] Republic of the Philippines, Office of the Press Secretary, "Speech by President Ferdinand Romualdez Marcos Jr. at the Meeting with Asia Society (with Q&A)," September 24, 2022.

[54] Gideon Rachman, "Ferdinand Marcos Jr Says Taiwan Tensions 'Very, Very Worrisome' for Philippines," *Financial Times*, January 18, 2023.

ment of Foreign Affairs followed suit, issuing a four-sentence statement that showed concern with cross-Strait tensions, reaffirmed Manila's One China policy, and urged restraint by all parties.[55] Other Philippine officials have emphasized the need to engage the United States and China on the issue to maintain the status quo. [56]

With no official relations with Taiwan and seeking to balance relations with China and the United States, promoting status quo policies is not easy for the Philippines. On one hand, the way that the United States engages Taiwan plays a very big role in how Manila engages Taiwan. According to one interviewee, as much as Manila is "as independent as it wants to be" on Taiwan, it is "limited in what [it] can do" and thus, practically, very much aligns itself with the direction that U.S. policy goes. And while Manila does not condone Chinese provocations against Taiwan, which one respondent called "disturbing," it is unable to directly confront Beijing. This leaves the Philippines to look to the United States to check Chinese actions. As interviewees noted, this is because China is the "same adversary" the Philippines faces.

The dilemma facing Manila is that, despite supporting U.S. pushback, they do not want the United States to push too hard for fear of that action leading to war. As one interviewee noted, there is a definite concern about Chinese activities around Taiwan that do necessitate some sort of counterforce, but that does not mean Manila wants the United States jumping in full-force or changing things up. Making things harder for Manila, according to interviewees, is that Philippine support can never be public, because officials do not want to say something that could give China a reason to "hit" the Philippines militarily or economically. Interviewees explained that these dynamics lead the Philippines to push publicly for both sides to tone down escalatory rhetoric as maintaining the status quo supports their interests in avoiding conflict.

---

[55] Department of Foreign Affairs (Republic of the Philippines), "Statement on Developments in Cross-Strait Relations," August 4, 2022.

[56] Vince Lopez and Macon Ramos-Araneta, "Carlos: We'll Be Neutral on Taiwan Issue," *Manila Standard News*, August 6, 2022; U.S. Department of State, 2022.

Philippine Views of Hypothetical Changes in U.S. Taiwan Policy

As discussed in Chapter 1, we conducted interviews in the Philippines in the fall of 2022, when the Marcos administration had just begun. We also monitored changes in Philippine policy that the Marcos administration adopted subsequently. Here, we discuss the interview responses and how we interpret them in light of recent developments.

Regardless of who is in power, Philippine leaders tend think about two countervailing pressures: maintaining strong relations between the United States, the Philippines' top security provider and treaty ally, and avoiding policies that could make the country a target of aggression from China, the Philippines' top economic partner. The country has a feeling of being "strategically straddled between the bitterly contested South China Sea and the Pacific Ocean, where competing interests of superpowers and other countries converge."[57] Given these considerations, the Philippines has a strong preference for the status quo in the Taiwan Strait. As one interviewee put it, the Philippines prefers that the United States, China, and Taiwan "not rock the boat."

Similar to what respondents said in Japan and the ROK, interviewees either did not care or were neutral about the trajectory of future intelligence ties between the United States and Taiwan, as they saw this as wholly a bilateral issue for Washington and Taipei. For one respondent, it was even a way to gauge U.S. commitment to the region. The same is true for policies in the economic domain, where there was strong support for the United States strengthening economic relations with Taiwan or supporting greater integration of Taiwan with other regional economies via the CPTPP, a move that one respondent called "a no-brainer." For both, there were largely negative views of Washington policies aimed at weakening those ties.

Philippine respondents were also largely neutral on the United States increasing arms sales to Taiwan. Respondents were not concerned about how arms sales to Taiwan might provoke or deter China. Rather, interview-

---

[57] Duterte, 2020; Rodrigo Roa Duterte, *National Security Strategy: Security and Development for Transformational Change and Well-Being of the Filipino People*, President of the Philippines, May 2018.

ees frequently stated that they wanted to be certain that increases in arms sales to Taiwan would also be paired with increases in arms sales to the Philippines.

In the diplomatic domain, Philippine respondents were more divided over which U.S. policies would support their preferred outcome of maintaining the status quo. Some respondents expressed support for U.S. efforts to increase advocacy for Taiwan's inclusion in the international arena that did not require statehood, for expanding high-level interactions, for the United States making more frequent statements to China regarding the "high costs" of moving against Taiwan, and for increasing references to Taiwan with other regional countries. As one respondent said, "It pains us to see Taiwan ostracized." In their view, these types of actions are reassuring because they show U.S. commitment—assuming that U.S. efforts go beyond just words but do not include any overt policy changes. For those who opposed such changes in U.S. diplomatic policy, the concern was that any of these changes could upset Beijing or represent the United States changing the status quo. The one change that saw the greatest consensus was if the U.S. explicitly stated that it would defend Taiwan. Respondents uniformly expressed concern for how Beijing would react and whether the United States would defend the Philippines should its rhetoric spark a conflict.

Interestingly, despite the mix in views regarding U.S. policies that signal a strengthening of ties with Taiwan, respondents showed more consensus in their reservations about policies that signaled a weakening of ties. Respondents expressed reservations about reductions in U.S. support to Taiwan in the diplomatic arena or in statements warning China from attacking Taiwan and about increases in the ambiguity of statements about the U.S. role to defend Taiwan. Although interviewees opposed Pelosi's visit, they did not support reductions in the frequency of other, less high-profile official interactions. Interviewees also opposed the United States reducing references to Taiwan in statements with other countries in the region. Interviewees tended to oppose a weakening of U.S. policies because, as best described by one respondent, Taiwan is viewed as a "barometer" for how the U.S. may respond to the Philippines. As another respondent replied, "We want the status quo. If [the] U.S. pulls back, it causes questions on U.S. commitment to its alliances." A separate respondent echoed this sentiment, saying that any U.S. weakening of its relations with Taiwan "could be seen as a litmus test of support to U.S. allies." Moreover, interviewees expressed concern that, should the United States weaken its engagement with Taiwan, China may take advantage of the situation. Similarly, one scholarly piece argues that the main security interest of the Philippines regarding Taiwan is "maintaining the status quo on Taiwan's political status" because any change could lead to conflict, which would be against Philippines' interests.[58]

This tendency to prefer the status quo is even more pronounced in respondents' answers to questions involving U.S. military options. While some believed the United States basing more air and naval forces in the region could better deter Chinese aggression, others feared further "militarization of the region," believing it could instead lead to conflict being more likely. Given the Philippine decision (subsequent to our interviews) to allow expanded U.S. access in the Philippines, however, we believe the former position to be more indicative of the perspective of the Marcos administration.

When asked about the United States increasing its presence in and around Taiwan, few respondents voiced support for such actions. Such actions were described as "destabilizing" and "escalatory," putting Manila in a position of feeling "jittery," concerned about "raising alarms in China," and worried that "China could retaliate." But this did not mean that the opposite policies were viewed favorably. Opposite actions (reducing U.S. presence, either regionally or around Taiwan, as well as reducing arms sales) also were received negatively. Reductions by the United States would "catch [our] attention" and cause "worry" because they would be viewed as a manifestation of the U.S. reducing its commitment to the region, which would be "destabilizing" and "disturbing" because it suggests the same could happen to the Philippines.

There remains the question of how the Philippines would respond if the United States were to reduce cooperation with Taiwan in this manner, a policy that our respondents noted would raise concerns about abandonment. There was no consensus on how Manila would approach such a situation. Some of our interviewees, speaking early in the Marcos administration, predicted that if the United States did decrease support to Taiwan, Manila might once again grow closer to the PRC. However, these respon-

---

[58] National Defense College of the Philippines, 2023.

dents did not anticipate the Marcos administration's emphasis on the U.S. alliance in the months that followed.

Moreover, historical precedent must be considered. Early in the Duterte regime, the Philippines sought to build closer ties with the PRC at the expense of its relationship with the United States. When Chinese aggression did not abate despite these overtures, however, the regime resumed closer ties with the United States. These seemingly divergent policies reinforce that the Philippines sees two options for responding to concerns about the threat China poses: drawing closer to China or strengthening ties with the United States. Which option the Philippines would be more likely to choose might depend on both the government in charge at the time and the strategic context, particularly the assertiveness of Chinese behavior.

Other respondents also noted that during the Trump administration, the Philippines prepared for the possibility of a more isolationist United States in multiple ways, including strengthening its relationships with both regional partners and extra-regional states, such as India. These respondents suggested that Manila might also seek to cooperate with Japan and South Korea, countries with disputes with China in the South China Sea, and emerging partners in South Asia, Oceania, and Europe. A reduction in U.S. support to Taiwan could lead to similar policies.

Conclusion

The Philippines' relations with the United States and China tend to be reflected in how it interacts with Taiwan. Because of Manila's tendency to balance its security ties with the United States with its economic ties with China, it seeks to preserve the status quo on all issues relating to Taiwan. Because of this, while Philippine respondents believed that the United States signaling commitment to Taiwan was a good sign for U.S. commitment to the Philippines, they feared that U.S. actions toward Taiwan could unnecessarily provoke China, which could lead to adverse impacts on the Philippines' security. For the Philippines, any action that could provoke China into some escalatory behavior is not desirable. Like the other cases, however, there was no interest in the United States seeking to limit its engagement with Taiwan, as this was interpreted as a signal of U.S. commitment to the region broadly and the Philippines more specifically. Finally, while Manila strongly supported the status quo, respondents viewed greater economic and intelligence engagement between the U.S. and Taiwan as completely uncontroversial. These views are summarized in Tables 5.1 and 5.2.

TABLE 5.1

The Philippines' Perspective on U.S. Options for Increasing Support to Taiwan

	U.S. Policy Option	The Philippines' Perspective
Diplomatic	Advocate for Taiwan's inclusion in fora that do not require statehood	Support
	Increase warnings directed at China about the costs of attacking Taiwan	Mixed feelings
	Increase emphasis on Taiwan in joint statements	Mixed feelings
	Increase high-level official interactions	Does not support
	Explicitly state that the United States will defend Taiwan	Does not support
Military	Increase regional presence	Support
	Increase arms sales and security assistance to Taiwan	Neutral
	Increase U.S. presence in or near Taiwan	Does not support
	Pursue a bilateral free trade agreement	Support
	Support Taiwan's inclusion in regional trade agreements	Support
	Increased intelligence sharing	Neutral

NOTE: Interviewees did not expect the government to support increasing U.S. regional presence. However, subsequent events have shown government support for more U.S. forces in the region.

TABLE 5.2

The Philippines' Perspective on U.S. Options for Decreasing Support to Taiwan

	U.S. Policy Option	The Philippines' Perspective
Diplomatic	Decrease high-level official interactions (e.g., Cabinet or senior congressional leaders)	Mixed feelings
	Decrease warnings to China about the costs of attacking Taiwan	Does not support
	Decrease emphasis on Taiwan in joint statements	Does not support
	Explicitly state that the United States will not defend Taiwan	Does not support
Military	Decrease regional presence	Does not support
	Decrease arms sales and security assistance	Does not support
	Decrease U.S. presence in or near Taiwan	Does not support
Economic and information	Reduce economic ties	Does not support
	Increased intelligence sharing	Neutral

CHAPTER 6

Findings

How might allies react to changes in U.S. policy toward Taiwan? In this chapter, we discuss similarities and differences in the ways Japan, the ROK, and the Philippines might respond in a near-term peacetime context. Significant shifts in the domestic political situation in each of these countries or in the international system, such as dramatic changes in China's or Taiwan's behavior, for example, could change the way that these states perceive and respond to future changes in U.S. policy.

Allies' Potential Reactions to Increased U.S. Support to Taiwan

Allies have some shared views and some divergent perspectives on U.S. options for increasing support to Taiwan (Table 6.1).

Japan Favors Increases in Many Forms of U.S. Diplomatic and Military Support to Taiwan and Would Adopt Similar Policies Up to a Point

Japan sees intrinsic value in preventing the PRC from controlling Taiwan, which could be used as a launching point for attacks on Japanese territory or for exerting control of waterways in the region. Further, Japan believes the possibility of a Chinese invasion of Taiwan is growing. Japan therefore strongly supports U.S. policies that signal a stronger commitment, which Japan believes will more effectively deter China and, failing that, prevent China from effectively gaining control of the island. Some commentators in Japan have expressed concerns that such policies could increase security

TABLE 6.1

Summary of Allies' Views on U.S. Options for Increasing Support to Taiwan

U.S. Policy Option		Ally's Perspective		
		Japan	ROK	The Philippines
Diplomatic	Advocate for Taiwan's inclusion in fora that do not require statehood	Support	Mixed feelings	Support
	Increase warnings directed at China about the costs of attacking Taiwan	Support	Mixed feelings	Mixed feelings
	Increase emphasis on Taiwan in joint statements	Support	Mixed feelings	Mixed feelings
	Increase high-level official interactions	Support	Does not support	Does not support
	Explicitly state that the United States will defend Taiwan	Mixed feelings	Does not support	Does not support
Military	Increase regional presence	Support	Mixed feelings	Support
	Increase arms sales and security assistance to Taiwan	Support	Mixed feelings	Neutral
	Increase U.S. presence in or near Taiwan	Mixed feelings	Mixed feelings	Does not support
	Pursue a bilateral free trade agreement	Support	Support	Support
	Support Taiwan's inclusion in regional trade agreements	Support	Support	Support
	Increased intelligence sharing	Neutral	Neutral	Neutral

NOTE: In the Philippines, interviewees did not expect the government to support increasing U.S. regional presence. However, subsequent events have shown government support for more U.S. forces in the region. Korean interviewees expected the government to support increases in regional presence, but disagreed on how the government would weigh China's response to increases in the ROK itself.

competition with China and make conflict more likely, but these views do not appear to be in the majority. Moreover, the Japanese officials we spoke with did not express such views, suggesting that concerns about provoking China do not affect government policy as much as they do in the Philippines and South Korea.

Interviewees in Japan strongly favor increased U.S. diplomatic support to Taiwan, though their responses suggest some limits. Generally, respondents supported more high-level visits and statements in support of Taiwan. Although some in Japan had concerns about the timing and lack of clear objectives of Pelosi's visit, they do not oppose high-level official visits generally. At the same time, there appear to be limits to how far they prefer the United States go. While some interviewees supported Biden's comments on U.S. willingness to defend Taiwan, they were not clamoring for the United States to go further, and others opposed a move toward strategic clarity. Generally, interviewees indicated that increasing U.S. diplomatic support to Taiwan makes it easier for Japan to follow suit, at least up to a point. Japan, for example, will likely not declare that Taiwan is a country or make a commitment to defend the island.

Regarding U.S. military policies, Japan generally favors more of everything: more U.S. forces in the region, more arms sales to and exercises with Taiwan, and more U.S. military presence near Taiwan, including freedom of navigation operations. All of these serve the purpose of deterring China from using force against Taiwan, which is a core Japanese interest. Interviewees, however, were concerned that putting U.S. forces on Taiwan would be excessively provocative.

The Philippines and the ROK Do Not Support Increasing Many Forms of U.S. Diplomatic and Military Support to Taiwan and Would Likely Not Adopt Such Policies Themselves

The Philippines and South Korea do not see Taiwan's status as a primary security concern. However, these countries do prioritize stability in the Taiwan Strait. A war would have adverse effects on both economies and, in the case of the ROK, potentially provide DPRK an opportunity to attack while U.S. forces are employed elsewhere. As a result of these views, the

ROK and the Philippines have different preferences for U.S. policy toward Taiwan than Japan does.

The ROK and the Philippines oppose highly publicized U.S. diplomatic support to Taiwan, which they believe increases tensions with China without strengthening the U.S. ability to deter China. Officials and analysts in both countries expressed concern about Biden's statements that the United States will defend Taiwan and Pelosi's visit to the island. Both countries were also opposed to an explicit U.S. commitment to Taiwan. Interviewees question whether such policies change China's beliefs about U.S. willingness to fight to defend Taiwan. Therefore, they are not convinced that these gestures increase the U.S. ability to deter China from attacking Taiwan. Moreover, interviewees noted that such policies provoke China to adopt militarized responses. This heightened level of military activity, in turn, increases the risk of conflict.

On military policies, the two countries had similar, but not entirely overlapping, views. Interviewees in the Philippines consistently opposed the United States increasing military activities on or around Taiwan, which they worried would provoke China, heighten security competition, and make conflict more likely. However, recent Philippine policies suggest that the Philippines does support increases in U.S. regional presence. In South Korea, officials and analysts shared these concerns about U.S. presence in and around Taiwan. However, ROK interviewees were more likely to note the importance of balancing two competing considerations: deterring China from attacking Taiwan and avoiding military actions that might provoke a series of events that could lead to war. Many in the ROK believed that increased arms sales to Taiwan and U.S. regional military presence could strike this balance.

Officials in the Philippines and South Korea appeared to have sought distance from the high-profile diplomatic events, such as Biden's statements and Pelosi's visit to Taiwan, favoring a return to the prior status quo. Were the United States to continue such actions and explicitly declare its support to Taiwan (without walking it back) or dramatically increase military support, it is unlikely that either country would publicly support such a change. It is, however, unclear whether more forceful U.S. policies would change either country's behavior in any other ways. For example, we are uncertain whether fear over an increasing risk of war over Taiwan and the possibility of their countries becoming a target would lead either country to change access arrangements for U.S. forces.

The Three Countries Are Neutral About Increased U.S. Intelligence Sharing and Supportive of Increases in U.S. Economic Relations with Taiwan

Interviewees in Japan, the Philippines, and South Korea were mildly supportive or ambivalent about hypothetical changes in U.S. intelligence sharing with Taiwan, seeing it as a bilateral issue. At the same time, there was unanimous support of hypothetical U.S. efforts to increase Taiwan's economic integration in the region. None of the allies feared that policy changes in the information and economic domains would significantly increase tensions with China.

Potential Responses to Reductions in U.S. Support to Taiwan

Those we interviewed in Japan, the ROK, and the Philippines found it difficult to imagine the United States downgrading its ties with Taiwan given current U.S. policy. Therefore, their answers to questions about such a scenario were more speculative, indicative of the expectation that the U.S. would remain committed to regional security. Their views are summarized in Table 6.2.

Japan, the ROK, and the Philippines Would See a Reduction in U.S. Support to Taiwan as a Signal of Waning U.S. Commitment to Their Security

Interviewees in all three allied countries indicated they would see reductions in U.S. diplomatic or military support to Taiwan as a signal about U.S. commitment to them. This finding is consistent with past analysis of alliance

TABLE 6.2

Summary of Allies' Views on U.S. Options for Decreasing Support to Taiwan

	U.S. Policy Option	Ally's Perspective		
		Japan	ROK	The Philippines
Diplomatic	Decrease high-level official interactions (e.g., Cabinet or senior congressional leaders)	Does not support	Mixed feelings	Mixed feelings
	Decrease warnings to China about the costs of attacking Taiwan	Does not support	Does not support	Does not support
	Decrease emphasis on Taiwan in joint statements	Does not support	Does not support	Does not support
	Explicitly state that the United States will not defend Taiwan	Does not support	Does not support	Does not support
Military	Decrease regional presence	Does not support	Does not support	Does not support
	Decrease arms sales and security assistance	Does not support	Does not support	Does not support
	Decrease U.S. presence in or near Taiwan	Does not support	Does not support	Does not support
Economic and information	Reduce economic ties	Does not support	Does not support	Does not support
	Increased intelligence sharing	Neutral	Neutral	Neutral

credibility.[1] However, it is notable because of important strategic differences between Taiwan and the three allies we discuss here. Most notably, Japan, the ROK, and the Philippines have mutual defense treaties with the United States. Such arrangements include an explicit U.S. promise to support these countries if attacked, something Taiwan no longer enjoys. The three allies see a strong linkage between U.S. commitment to Taiwan and U.S. commitment to their security, despite this and other key differences (e.g., historical relationship with and proximity to mainland China). For Japan, at least, an important similarity with Taiwan—China as a shared security challenge—explains the linkage. Interviewees in Japan worried that a U.S. decision not to defend Taiwan would be a harbinger of a U.S. decision not to defend Japanese territory, including claims to the Senkaku Islands.

These Allies Oppose Reductions in U.S. Support to Taiwan, Which They Believe Might Lead to Instability in the Taiwan Strait

Interviewees in Japan, the ROK, and the Philippines all oppose a reduction in U.S. support to Taiwan. This is, in part, as noted above, because they see a link between U.S. commitment to Taiwan and U.S. commitment to themselves. However, this is not their only motivation. All three countries have an interest in stability in the Taiwan Strait and see the possibility of U.S. defense of Taiwan as an important part of deterring a PRC attack on the island. Japan's opposition would likely be strongest, because it believes that PRC control of Taiwan would pose a significant security challenge for the Japanese homeland.

---

[1] Jonathan Mercer, *Reputation and International Politics*, Cornell University Press, 1996.

The Value Japan and the ROK Place on Their Alliances with the United States Suggests That Concerns About U.S. Reliability Would Lead Them to First Try to Draw the U.S. Closer

Interviewees were not explicit about how their governments would react to a reduction in U.S. support to Taiwan over their objections. Still, these discussions offer insights into these allies' most likely courses of action. Our interviews reinforced government statements about Japan's and the ROK's deep security concerns about China and North Korea, respectively. Interviewees also reiterated that both governments see their alliances with the United States as fundamental to their security. As a result, Japan's and the ROK's initial response to heightened fear about U.S. abandonment would likely be to try to pull the United States, their current security provider, closer. There was no indication that Japan would consider building closer ties with China, and significant doubt that this was a plausible course of action for the ROK to maintain its security, since interviewees stated that China's influence on the DPRK alone cannot ensure Korea's security.

Of course, our interviewees discussed how states could also respond to concerns about U.S. reliability by spending more on their own defense or by forming stronger security partnerships with other states that fear China's growing power. Beyond these broad impressions from our discussions in each country, it is difficult to make more concrete conclusions. Therefore, we recommend more detailed analysis of each country's policy options and how they would rate these alternatives.

Past Behavior Suggests That the Philippines' Response to Concerns About U.S. Reliability Would Depend on Who Is in Power and China's Recent Behavior

Currently, despite close economic ties, the Philippines sees China as a significant security challenge and appears likely to try to draw the United States closer if the Philippines feared abandonment due to changes in U.S. policy toward Taiwan. However, some past Philippine leaders have attempted closer relations with China in periods when China's behavior was less assertive. Concerns about U.S. abandonment could once again make such a policy attractive. Therefore, we assess that Philippine responses to concerns about U.S. reliability may depend more on the context, specifically who is leading the Philippines and China's recent behavior.

Final Thoughts

Our findings have implications for U.S. policymakers considering whether and how to change U.S. policy toward Taiwan. U.S. treaty allies have a direct stake in U.S. actions vis-à-vis Taiwan. U.S. policymakers should therefore expect these countries to react to any U.S. policy changes toward Taiwan and consider how those reactions affect U.S. regional interests. In other words, allies' reactions should be part of the broader assessment of the trade-offs associated with changes in U.S. policy toward Taiwan that would also consider other factors, such as effects on China's and Taiwan's behavior.

The debate in the United States about U.S. policy toward Taiwan has been overtaken by a narrow discussion over the value of retaining strategic ambiguity versus a shift to strategic clarity. There is, however, a much broader—and richer—discussion to be had over the policy options the United States has for signaling closer or weaker ties with Taiwan, how allies would respond to each option, and whether allies would follow suit by adopting similar policies.

If the United States wishes to signal a firmer commitment to Taiwan, it has multiple ways of doing so. Allies may respond differently depending on what policy tool the United States employs to send that message. Allies are likely to support increases in bilateral economic ties and to be neutral about stronger intelligence ties between the United States and Taiwan. However, allies would likely have more divergent responses to increases in diplomatic or military support by the United States to Taiwan. In specific reference to the debate in Washington over clarity versus ambiguity, all three allies have concerns about proposals for the United States to explicitly and unambiguously commit to Taiwan's defense and would not likely follow the U.S. lead by adopting such policies themselves.

If a future administration were to consider reducing support to Taiwan, allies would not support a change in policy and would not likely follow the U.S. lead by decreasing their own support to Taiwan. Moreover, the United States should expect allies to be deeply concerned about the U.S. commitment to them. We suggest that, at least at present, concerns about U.S. reliability would lead allies to seek closer relations with the United States. A weakening of U.S.-Taiwan ties could also result in an increase in allies' defense spending, which the United States has been long promoting. At the same time, under certain conditions, the Philippines may be more likely to cooperate or settle disputes with China in ways that the United States opposes. Given the importance of these responses and remaining uncertainties about how allies' views may evolve in the future, more research is needed on allies' potential response to the United States downgrading ties with Taiwan.

This is ultimately a snapshot of allied perspectives on U.S. policy options in the current strategic setting. If the United States decides to pursue changes in policy toward Taiwan in a substantially different setting, it will need to consider allied views once again. Significant changes in China's, Taiwan's, and the United States' behavior and power are among the factors that might alter how allies respond to the prospect of changing U.S.-Taiwan relations.

Even as the strategic setting changes, one thing will remain the same: Allies' potential reactions could affect U.S. interests and therefore should be considered as a factor in U.S. policymaking on Taiwan. Our analysis highlights the diversity of views among allies and the possibility that they may have different opinions on and reactions to changes in U.S. policy. Understanding the policies that are likely to provoke the strongest support and strongest opposition among U.S. allies enables policymakers to recognize the most likely areas to reach consensus and those that will require significant discussions or potentially create larger trade-offs. While it is true that the three countries currently share a concern about Chinese power, we cannot assume that their reliance on the United States for their security means that they will follow any policy that Washington chooses to pursue.

Abbreviations

AFP	Armed Forces of the Philippines
CPTPP	Comprehensive and Progressive Agreement for Trans-Pacific Partnership
DPRK	Democratic People's Republic of Korea
EDCA	Enhanced Defense Cooperation Agreement
NATO	North Atlantic Treaty Organization
PRC	People's Republic of China
ROC	Republic of China
ROK	Republic of Korea
THAAD	terminal high altitude area defense
TRA	Taiwan Relations Act
TSEA	Taiwan Security Enhancement Act
UN	United Nations
VFA	Visiting Forces Agreement

References

"Abe Congratulates Tsai on Election as Taiwan's President," *Japan Times*, January 18, 2016. As of February 22, 2023:
https://www.japantimes.co.jp/news/2016/01/18/national/politics-diplomacy/abe-congratulates-tsai-on-election-as-taiwans-president/

Abe Shinzō, "Keynote Speech/Impact Forum" ["キーノートスピーチ / インパクト・フォーラム"], Institute for National Policy Research [國策研究院], video, December 1, 2021. As of February 22, 2023:
https://www.youtube.com/watch?v=qkwCMattztQ

Alles, Delphine, Auriane Guilbaud, and Delphine Lagrange, "Interviews in International Relations," in Guillaume Devin, ed., *Resources and Applied Methods in International Relations*, Springer, 2018.

American Presidency Project, "William J. Clinton Press Briefing by Mike McCurry," March 12, 1996. As of February 2, 2023:
https://www.presidency.ucsb.edu/documents/press-briefing-mike-mccurry-298

Asia Briefing, "Taiwan and the Philippines Work to Enhance Trade Ties," webpage, undated.

Ashley, Ryan, "Japan's Revolution on Taiwan Affairs," *War on the Rocks*, 2021. As of December 1, 2022:
https://warontherocks.com/2021/11/japans-revolution-on-taiwan-affairs/

Banlaoi, Rommel C., "[Opinion] Flexible Foreign Policy: Balancing PH Relations with US, China Under Marcos Jr. Presidency," Rappler.com, October 19, 2022. As of February 3, 2023:
https://www.rappler.com/voices/thought-leaders/opinion-flexible-foreign-policy-balancing-philippine-relations-united-states-china-marcos-presidency/

Bernkopf Tucker, Nancy, *Strait Talk: United States–Taiwan Relations and the Crisis with China*, Harvard University Press, 2011.

Berry, Jeffrey M., "Validity and Reliability Issues in Elite Interviewing," *PS: Political Science & Politics*, Vol. 35, No. 4, 2002.

Biden, Joseph R., Jr., "Not So Deft on Taiwan," *Washington Post*, May 2, 2001.

"Biden Tells 60 Minutes U.S. Troops Would Defend Taiwan, but White House Says This Is Not Official U.S. Policy," CBS News, September 18, 2022.

Branigin, William, "U.S. Military Ends Role in Philippines," *Washington Post*, November 24, 1992.

"Bush Pledges Whatever It Takes to Defend Taiwan," CNN, April 25, 2001.

Bush, Richard C., "A One-China Policy Primer," Brookings Institution, East Asia Policy Paper 10, Vol. 10, 2017.

Bush, Richard C., *At Cross Purposes: U.S.-Taiwan Relations Since 1942*, Taylor & Francis Group, 2015.

Cairo Declaration, U.S. Department of State Bulletin, 1943.

Calonzo, Andreo, and Cecilia Yap, "China Visit Helps Duterte Reap Funding Deals Worth $24 Billion," Bloomberg, October 21, 2016.

Campbell, Caitlin, and Susan L. Lawrence, *Taiwan: Political and Security Issues*, Congressional Research Service, 2022.

Carpenter, Ted Galen, and Eric Gomez, "East Asia and a Strategy of Restraint," *War on the Rocks*, August 10, 2016. As of May 19, 2021: https://warontherocks.com/2016/08/east-asia-and-a-strategy-of-restraint/

Castillo, Jasen J., "Passing the Torch: Criteria for Implementing a Grand Strategy of Offshore Balancing," in Richard Fontaine and Loren DeJonge Schulman, eds., *New Voices in Grand Strategy*, Center for a New American Security, 2019.

Cha, Victor, *Powerplay: The Origins of the American Alliance System in Asia*, Princeton University Press, 2016.

Chang, Parris H., "The Taiwan-PRC Competition on the Korean Peninsula," *Korean Journal of Defense Analysis*, Vol. 13, No. 1, 2001.

"China Unhappy as Philippines Signs Investment Deal with Taiwan," Reuters, December 8, 2017.

Christensen, Thomas J, *Useful Adversaries: Grand Strategy, Domestic Mobilization, and Sino-American Conflict, 1947–1958*, Vol. 179, Princeton University Press, 1996.

CNN Philippines Staff, "'PH Won't Lose an Inch of Its Territory,' Says Marcos," CNN Philippines, February 18, 2023. As of March 22, 2023: https://www.cnnphilippines.com/news/2023/2/18/ph-wont-lose-inch-of-territory-marcos.html

Cruz de Castro, Renato, "Can the Philippines Stay Neutral in a Taiwan Strait Military Confrontation Between the US and China?" *Think China*, October 5, 2022. As of February 3, 2023: https://www.thinkchina.sg/can-philippines-stay-neutral-taiwan-strait-military-confrontation-between-us-and-china

Cruz de Castro, Renato, "Duterte Finally Admits the Importance of the U.S. Alliance," Asia Maritime Transparency Initiative, February 24, 2021. As of February 3, 2023: https://amti.csis.org/duterte-finally-admits-the-importance-of-the-u-s-alliance/

Davies, Philip H. J., "Spies as Informants: Triangulation and the Interpretation of Elite Interview Data in the Study of the Intelligence and Security Services," *Politics*, Vol. 21, No. 1, 2001.

deLisle, Jacques, *U.S.-Japan-Taiwan Dialogue: Deterrence, Defense, and Trilateral Cooperation*, Foreign Policy Research Institute, December 12, 2022.

Department of Foreign Affairs (Republic of the Philippines), *National Defense Strategy 2018–2022*, November 1, 2018. As of February 3, 2023:
https://www.globalsecurity.org/military/library/report/2018/philippines-national-defense-strategy_2018-2022_201811.pdf

Department of Foreign Affairs (Republic of the Philippines), "Statement on Developments in Cross-Strait Relations," August 4, 2022. As of May 18, 2023:
https://dfa.gov.ph/dfa-news/statements-and-advisoriesupdate/30944-statement-on-developments-in-cross-strait-relations

Di, He, "'The Last Campaign to Unify China': The CCP'S Unmaterialized Plan to Liberate Taiwan, 1949–1950," *Chinese Historians*, Vol. 5, No. 1, 1992.

Doce, Brian, "People-Centric Diplomacy and Philippine-Taiwan Relations," *Facts Asia*, November 30, 2021. As of February 23, 2023:
https://www.factsasia.org/blog/people-centric-diplomacy-and-philippine-taiwan-relations

Doshi, Rush, *The Long Game: China's Grand Strategy and the Displacement of American Order*, Oxford University Press, 2021.

Dossani, Rafiq, "The Biden-Moon Meetings: Much Ado About Something?" *RAND Blog*, June 4, 2021. As of February 3, 2023:
https://www.rand.org/blog/2021/06/the-biden-moon-meetings-much-ado-about-something.html

"Duterte Cancels Order to Terminate VFA with US," CNN Philippines, July 30, 2021. As of February 3, 2023:
https://www.cnnphilippines.com/news/2021/7/30/Visiting-Forces-Agreement-Philippines-United-States-Duterte-Austin.html

Duterte, Rodrigo Roa, "Speech During the Philippines-China Trade and Investment Forum," Speech, Beijing, China, October 20, 2016.

Duterte, Rodrigo Roa, "National Security Policy for Change and Well-Being of the Filipino People," Philippine Department of National Defense, April 1, 2017.

Duterte, Rodrigo Roa, *National Security Strategy: Security and Development for Transformational Change and Well-Being of the Filipino People*, President of the Philippines, May 2018.

Duterte, Rodrigo Roa, "5th State of the Nation Address," Session Hall of the Filipino House of Representatives, July 27, 2020a.

Duterte, Rodrigo Roa, "Full Text: President Duterte's Speech at the 75th UN General Assembly," Rappler.com, September 23, 2020b. As of February 3, 2023:
https://www.rappler.com/nation/full-text-duterte-unga-speech-2020

Eisenhower, Dwight D., "Letter from President Eisenhower to British Prime Minister Churchill, January 25, 1955, in U.S. Department of State, Office of the Historian, *Foreign Relations of the United States*, 1955–1957, Vol. 2, Document 41.

Espeña, Joshua Bernard, "A 'Taiwan Dilemma' for the Philippines," Atlas Institute for International Affairs, September 26, 2020.

Fearon, James D., "Rationalist Explanations for War," *International Organization*, Vol. 49, No. 3, 1995.

Feigenbaum, Evan A., and Barbara Weisel, "Deepening the U.S.-Taiwan Economic Partnership," Carnegie Endowment for International Peace, March 4, 2021.

Formosa Resolution—*See* Public Law 84-4.

"Full Transcript of ABC News' George Stephanopoulos' Interview with President Joe Biden," ABC News, August 19, 2021. As of February 2, 2023:
https://abcnews.go.com/Politics/full-transcript-abc-news-george-stephanopoulos-interview-president/story?id=79535643

Garver, John W., *Face Off: China, the United States, and Taiwan's Democratization*, University of Washington Press, 2011.

Garver, John W., *The Sino-American Alliance: Nationalist China and American Cold War Strategy in Asia*, M. E. Sharpe, 1999.

Gentile, Gian, Yvonne K. Crane, Dan Madden, Timothy M. Bonds, Bruce W. Bennett, Michael J. Mazarr, and Andrew Scobell, *Four Problems on the Korean Peninsula: North Korea's Expanding Nuclear Capabilities Drive a Complex Set of Problems*, RAND Corporation, TL-271-A, 2019. As of February 9, 2023:
https://www.rand.org/pubs/tools/TL271.html

George, Alexander L., and Richard Smoke, *Deterrence in American Foreign Policy: Theory and Practice*, Columbia University Press, 1974.

Glaser, Bonnie S., Michael J. Mazarr, Michael J. Glennon, Richard Haass, and David Sacks, "Dire Straits: Should American Support for Taiwan Be Ambiguous?" *Foreign Affairs*, Vol. 24, 2020.

Glaser, Bonnie S., "A Guarantee Isn't Worth the Risk," *Foreign Affairs*, September 24, 2020.

Glaser, Bonnie S., and Charmaine Willoughby, "China's Relations with the Philippines Under Ferdinand 'BongBong' Marcos, Jr.," *China Global Podcast*, 2022. As of February 3, 2023:
https://www.gmfus.org/news/
chinas-relations-philippines-under-ferdinand-bongbong-marcos-jr

Glaser, Charles L., "A U.S.-China Grand Bargain? The Hard Choice between Military Competition and Accommodation," *International Security*, Vol. 39, No. 4, 2015.

Glennon, John P., and S. Everett Gleason, eds. *Foreign Relations of the United States, 1950, Korea*, Vol. VII, U.S. Government Printing Office, 1976.

Glennon, John P., David W. Mabon, and Harriet D. Schwar, eds., *Foreign Relations of the United States, 1952–1954, China and Japan*, Vol. XIV, Part 1, U.S. Government Printing Office, 1985.

Gold, Martin B., *A Legislative History of the Taiwan Relations Act: Bridging the Strait*, Lexington Books, 2016.

Goldstein, Lyle J., "How Progressives and Restrainers Can Unite on Taiwan and Reduce the Potential for Conflict with China," *Responsible Statecraft*, April 17, 2020.

Goldwater v. Carter, 444 U.S. 996, 1979.

Gomez, Jim, "Marcos Says Sea Feud Involving China Keeps Him Up at Night," AP News, January 19, 2023.

Gomez, Jim, "Philippines Says US on Its Own in South China Sea Patrols," *Philippine Star*, December 8, 2016.

Gomez, Jim, and Joeal Calupitan, "Marcos Jr. Reaffirms US Ties in First 100 days of Presidency," AP News, October 7, 2022.

Government of Japan, *National Defense Strategy*, translated by Ministry of Defense of Japan (provisional translation as of December 28, 2022), December 16, 2022a. As of February 9, 2023:
https://www.mod.go.jp/j/approach/agenda/guideline/strategy/pdf/
strategy_en.pdf

Government of Japan, *National Security Strategy of Japan*, provisional translation, December 16, 2022b. As of February 9, 2023:
https://www.cas.go.jp/jp/siryou/221216anzenhoshou/nss-e.pdf

Government Public Relations Cabinet Office (Japan), "Public Poll on Diplomacy" ["外交に関する世論調査"], 2003–2023. As of February 22, 2023:
https://survey.gov-online.go.jp/index-gai.html

Government Public Relations Cabinet Office (Japan), "Japan and China" ["日本と中国"], "Summary of the Public Poll on Diplomacy" ["外交に関する世論調査 の概要"], February 13, 2023. As of February 21, 2023:
https://survey.gov-online.go.jp/r04/r04-gaiko/gairyaku.pdf

Grossman, Derek, "China Has Lost the Philippines Despite Duterte's Best Efforts," *Foreign Policy*, May 3, 2021.

Haass, Richard, and David Sacks, "American Support for Taiwan Must Be Unambiguous: To Keep the Peace, Make Clear to China That Force Won't Stand," *Foreign Affairs*, September 2, 2020.

Haenle, Paul, and Evan Medeiros, "Why the U.S. Needs to Say Less and Do More on Taiwan," Carnegie Endowment for International Peace, July 18, 2022.

Halperin, Morton H, *The 1958 Taiwan Straits Crisis: A Documented History*, RAND Corporation, RM-4900-ISA, 1966. As of May 18, 2023:
https://www.rand.org/pubs/research_memoranda/RM4900.html

Harold, Scott W., Derek Grossman, Brian Harding, Jeffrey W. Hornung, Gregory Poling, Jeffrey Smith, and Meagan L. Smith, *The Thickening Web of Asian Security Cooperation: Deepening Defense Ties Among U.S. Allies and Partners in the Indo-Pacific*, RAND Corporation, RR-3125-MCF, 2019. As of February 22, 2023:
https://www.rand.org/pubs/research_reports/RR3125.html

Harris, Tobias, and Levi McLaughlin, "The Small Pacifist Party That Could Shape Japan's Future," *Foreign Policy*, November 4, 2021.

Henry, Iain D., *Reliability and Alliance Interdependence: The United States and Its Allies in Asia, 1949–1969*, Cornell University Press, 2022.

Heydarian, Richard Javad, "Duterte's Uncertain China Gamble," Asia Maritime Transparency Initiative, November 3, 2016.

Heydarian, Richard Javad, "Foreign Policy Under Marcos Jr.: More Like Father Than Outgoing Duterte," Asia Maritime Transparency Initiative, June 13, 2022.

Hornung, Jeffrey W., "Abe Shinzō's Lasting Impact: Proactive Contributions to Japan's Security and Foreign Policies," *Asia-Pacific Review*, Vol. 28, No. 1, 2021.

Hornung, Jeffrey W., *Japan's Potential Contributions in an East China Sea Contingency*, RAND Corporation, RR-A34-1, 2020. As of February 22, 2023:
https://www.rand.org/pubs/research_reports/RRA314-1.html

Hornung, Jeffrey W., "Japan's Long-Awaited Return to Geopolitics," *Foreign Policy*, February 6, 2023.

Hornung, Jeffrey W., *Learning How to Sweat: Explaining the Dispatch of Japan's Self-Defense Forces in the Gulf War and Iraq War*, Columbian College of Arts and Sciences of the George Washington University, dissertation, UMI No. 3366728, August 31, 2009.

Hornung, Jeffrey W., "Strong but Constrained Japan-Taiwan Ties," Brookings, March 13, 2018.

Hung, Jason, "China's Soft Power Grows in the Philippines," *The Diplomat*, February 26, 2021.

Joint Communiqué of the Government of the People's Republic of China and the Government of the Republic of the Philippines, June 9, 1975.

Joint Communiqué of the United States of America and the People's Republic of China (Shanghai Communiqué), February 28, 1972.

Joint Communiqué of the United States of America and the People's Republic of China (Normalization Communiqué), January 1, 1979.

Joint Communiqué of the United States of America and the People's Republic of China (Arms Sales Communiqué), August 17, 1982.

Joint Statement of the United States and Japan, January 13, 2023. As of February 22, 2023:
https://www.whitehouse.gov/briefing-room/statements-releases/2023/01/13/joint-statement-of-the-united-states-and-japan

Kanno-Youngs, Zolan, and Peter Baker, "Biden Pledges to Defend Taiwan if It Faces a Chinese Attack," *New York Times*, May 23, 2022.

Kim, Bo-gyung, "South Korea–China Trade Volume Rises to Pre-THAAD Levels," *Korea Herald*, December 19, 2018.

Kim, Seung-Young, "Nationalism and the Pursuit of Nuclear Weapons and Missiles: The South Korean Case, 1970-82," *Diplomacy & Statecraft*, Vol. 12, No. 4, 2001.

Kim, Soo, "Takeaways from the Biden-Moon Summit: Three Observations on China," *RAND Blog*, June 7, 2021. As of February 3, 2023:
https://www.rand.org/blog/2021/06/takeaways-from-the-biden-moon-summit-three-observations.html

"Komeito Head Yamaguchi Seeks to Visit China in January and Build Bridges, Some in Ruling Party Object" ["公明・山口代表、1月の中国訪問模索　橋渡し狙い、与党内で異論も"], *Mainichi Shimbun*, December 22, 2022. As of February 21, 2023:
https://mainichi.jp/articles/20221222/k00/00m/010/306000c

"Korea's Food Exports to China Slide in March over THAAD Row," *Korea Herald*, April 4, 2017.

Koya, Chida, "Komeito Seals Its 'Pro-China' Image, Takes Pride in Its Role as Bridge-Builder While Criticizing an Exercise" ["公明「親中」イメージ封印 橋渡し役自負も演習は批判"], *Sankei Shimbun*, August 17, 2022. As of February 21, 2023:
https://www.sankei.com/
article/20220817-7RJTWVM63NPJBHH5H5GD5K2574/

Kuo, Raymond, "'Strategic Ambiguity' Has the U.S. and Taiwan Trapped," *Foreign Policy*, January 18, 2023.

Lee, Ji-Young, *The Geopolitics of South Korea–China Relations: Implications for U.S. Policy in the Indo-Pacific*, RAND Corporation, PE-A524-1, 2020. As of February 3, 2023:
https://www.rand.org/pubs/perspectives/PEA524-1.html

Lee, Michael, "Koreans Are Growing Much Less Fond of China," *Korea JoongAng Daily*, August 22, 2022a.

Lee, Seong-Hyon, "South Korean Angle on the Taiwan Strait: Familiar Issue, Unfamiliar Option," Stimson Center, policy memo, February 23, 2022b.

Library of Congress, Federal Research Division, "Country Studies: Relations with Asian Neighbors," webpage, undated. As of February 9, 2023:
http://countrystudies.us/philippines/93.htm

Liff, Adam P., "Has Japan's Policy Toward the Taiwan Strait Changed?" *Washington Post*, August 18, 2021.

Liptak, Kevin, "Biden Vows to Protect Taiwan in Event of Chinese Attack," CNN, October 22, 2021.

Liu, Hong, "The Sino-South Korean Normalization: A Triangular Explanation," *Asian Survey*, Vol. 33, No. 11, November 1, 1993.

Lopez, Vince, and Macon Ramos-Araneta, "Carlos: We'll Be Neutral on Taiwan Issue," *Manila Standard News*, August 6, 2022.

Lum, Thomas, and Ben Dolven, *The Republic of the Philippines and U.S. Interests—2014*, Congressional Research Service, May 15, 2014. As of February 24, 2023:

Luria, Elaine, "Congress Must Untie Biden's Hands on Taiwan," *Washington Post*, October 11, 2021.

Manyin, Mark E., Caitlin Campbell, Emma Chanlett-Avery, Mary Beth D. Nikitin, and Brock R. Williams, *U.S.–South Korea Relations*, Congressional Research Service, R41481, updated February 24, 2022.

Maritime Awareness Project, *Philippines*, National Bureau of Asian Research, undated. As of February 24, 2023:
https://www.nbr.org/publication/philippines/

Matsuda, Yasuhiro, "Cross-Strait Relations Under the Ma Ying-jeou Administration: From Economic to Political Dependence?" *Journal of Contemporary East Asia Studies*, Vol. 4, No. 2, 2015.

Mazarr, Michael J., Bryan Frederick, John J. Drennan, Emily Ellinger, Kelly Elizabeth Eusebi, Bryan Rooney, Andrew Stravers, and Emily Yoder, *Understanding Influence in the Strategic Competition with China*, RAND Corporation, RR-A290-1, 2021. As of February 3, 2023:
https://www.rand.org/pubs/research_reports/RRA290-1.html

Meick, Ethan, and Nargiza Salidjanova, *China's Response to U.S.-South Korean Missile Defense System Deployment and Its Implications*, U.S.-China Economic and Security Review Commission, 2017.

Mercene, Recto, "US Official: Military Aid to PHL Still Priority," *Business Monitor*, November 8, 2019.

Mercer, Jonathan, *Reputation and International Politics*, Cornell University Press, 1996.

Ministry of Defense (Japan), *Defense of Japan*, 2022a.

Ministry of Defense (Japan), *Defense Buildup Plan* ["「防 衛 力 整 備 計 画」"], December 16, 2022b. As of February 23, 2023:
https://www.mod.go.jp/j/approach/agenda/guideline/plan/pdf/plan.pdf

Ministry of Foreign Affairs (Japan), *Diplomatic Bluebook 2022*, 2022. As of February 22, 2023:
https://www.mofa.go.jp/policy/other/bluebook/2022/pdf/pdfs/2022_all.pdf

Ministry of Foreign Affairs (Republic of China), "Republic of China (Taiwan) Signs Fisheries Agreement with Japan," press release, 2020. As of December 1, 2022:
https://www.mofa.gov.tw/en/News_Content.aspx?n=539A9A50A5F8AF9E&sms=37B41539382B84BA&s=E80C25D078D837BB

Ministry of Foreign Affairs (Republic of China), "ROC Congratulates Philippines on Conclusion of Its General Elections," May 12, 2016. As of February 3, 2023:
https://en.mofa.gov.tw/News_Content.aspx?n=1328&sms=273&s=33818

Ministry of Foreign Affairs (Republic of China), "Taiwan-Philippines Relations," February 20, 2013. As of February 3, 2023:
https://www.roc-taiwan.org/ph_en/post/66.html

Mogato, Manuel, "Philippines' Duterte Wants to 'Open Alliances' with Russia, China," Reuters, September 26, 2016.

Mosley, Layna, "Introduction: 'Just Talk to People'? Interviews in Contemporary Political Science," in Layna Mosely, ed., *Interview Research in Political Science*, Cornell University Press, 2013.

Mutual Defense Treaty Between the United States and the Republic of China, December 2, 1954.

National Archives, "The President's News Conference," Harry S. Truman Library, January 5, 1950. As of February 2, 2023:
https://www.trumanlibrary.gov/library/public-papers/3/presidents-news-conference

National Archives, "News Conference 37, June 27, 1962," JFK Library, June 27, 1962. As of February 2, 2023:
https://www.jfklibrary.org/archives/other-resources/john-f-kennedy-press-conferences/news-conference-37

National Defense College of the Philippines, "Philippine Foreign Policy and the Complexities of Cross-Strait Relations," February 6, 2023. As of February 3, 2023:
https://www.ndcp.edu.ph/philippine-foreign-policy-and-the-complexities-of-cross-strait-relations/#_edn9

National Foreign Assessment Center, "South Korea: Nuclear Developments and Strategic Decisionmaking," June 1, 1978. As of February 3, 2023:
https://nautilus.org/wp-content/uploads/2011/09/CIA_ROK_Nuclear_DecisionMaking.pdf

Oberdorfer, Don, and Robert Carlin, *The Two Koreas: A Contemporary History*, Basic Books, 1997.

Observatory of Economic Complexity, "Japan," webpage, undated-a. As of February 24, 2023:
https://oec.world/en/profile/country/jpn?yearlyTradeFlowSelector=flow1

Observatory of Economic Complexity, "South Korea Exports Data," webpage, undated-b. As of February 3, 2023:
https://oec.world/en/profile/country/kor?subnationalTimeSelector=timeYear&subnationalFlowSelector=flow1

Observatory of Economic Complexity, "Philippines," webpage, August 1, 2021. As of February 3, 2023:
https://oec.world/en/profile/country/phl?yearlyTradeFlowSelector=flow1

Ogata, Sadako, *Normalization with China: A Comparative Study of U.S. and Japanese Processes*, Institute of East Asian Studies, University of California, 1988.

Okinawa Prefectural Government, "What Okinawa Wants You to Understand About the U.S. Military Bases," March 1, 2018. As of February 22, 2023:
https://dc-office.org/wp-content/uploads/2018/03/E-all.pdf

Olsen, Henry, "Biden Is Right on Taiwan. Now He Needs a Staff That Won't Undercut Him," *Washington Post*, September 19, 2022.

References

Pang, Yang Huei, *Strait Rituals: China, Taiwan, and the United States in the Taiwan Strait Crisis, 1954–1958*, Hong Kong University Press, 2019.

Park, Ju-min, "Japan Official, Calling Taiwan 'Red Line,' Urges Biden to 'Be Strong,'" Reuters, December 25, 2020a.

Park, Junghyun, "Frustrated Alignment: The Pacific Pact Proposals from 1949 to 1954 and South Korea–Taiwan Relations," *International Journal of Asian Studies*, Vol. 12, No. 2, 2015.

Park, Young Kil, "The Role of Fishing Disputes in China–South Korea Relations," Maritime Awareness Project, April 23, 2020b. As of February 3, 2023:
https://map.nbr.org/wp-content/uploads/2020/09/analysis_park_42320.pdf

Parker, Ashley, Marianna Sotomayor, and Isaac Stanley-Becker, "Inside the Republican Drift Away from Supporting the NATO Alliance," *Washington Post*, April 29, 2022.

Petersen, Neal H., William Z. Slany, Charles S. Sampson, John P. Glennon, and David W. Mabon, eds. *Foreign Relations of the United States, 1950, East Asia and the Pacific*, Vol. VI, Document 183, U.S. Government Printing Office, 1976.

Philippine Consulate General in Xiamen China, "About Us: Historical Background," undated. As of May 18, 2023:
https://xiamenpcg.dfa.gov.ph/about-us/historical-background-new

Philippine Representative Office in Taiwan, Manila Economic and Cultural Office, "Who We Are," webpage, undated. As of February 3, 2023:
https://www.meco.org.tw/about-us

"Philippines' Duterte Would Send Navy Ships in South China Sea to Assert Claim over Resources," Reuters, April 19, 2021.

Pickrell, Ryan, "Firebrand Philippine President Pushes the US to Send the Entire 7th Fleet Into the South China Sea," *Business Insider*, July 8, 2019.

Porter, Patrick, "The United States Should Not Defend Taiwan," *National Review*, December 20, 2021.

Posen, Barry R., *Restraint: A New Foundation for U.S. Grand Strategy*, Cornell University Press, 2014.

"Possibility of Taiwan Emergency 'Existence Crisis Situation' Deputy Prime Minister Aso [「"台湾有事「存立危機事態」にあたる可能性" 麻生副総理」]," *NHK*, 2021. As of December 1, 2022:
https://www.nhk.or.jp/politics/articles/statement/63108.html

President of the Philippines, Executive Order 313, "Prohibiting Philippine Government Officials to Visit Taiwan or to Receive Calls by Visiting Taiwanese Officials," signed December 17, 1987.

Public Law 84-4, The Formosa Resolution (Joint Resolution Authorizing the President to employ the Armed Forces of the United States for Protecting the Security of Formosa, the Pescadores and Related Positions and Territories of that Area), January 29, 1955.

Public Law 96-8, Taiwan Relations Act, April 10, 1979.

Public Law 117-263, National Defense Authorization Act for Fiscal Year 2023, December 7, 2022.

Rachman, Gideon, "Ferdinand Marcos Jr Says Taiwan Tensions 'Very, Very Worrisome' for Philippines," *Financial Times*, January 18, 2023.

Reid, John G., and John P. Glennon, eds., *Foreign Relations of the United States, 1949, The Far East and Australasia*, Vol. VII, Part 2, Document 387, U.S. Government Printing Office, 1976.

Republic of Korea, *Strategy for a Free, Peaceful, and Prosperous Indo-Pacific Region*, 2022.

Republic of the Philippines, Presidential Memorandum Circular No. 148, "Prescribing the Guidelines for the Implementation of Executive Order No. 313," 1987.

Republic of the Philippines, Office of the Press Secretary, "Speech by President Ferdinand Romualdez Marcos Jr. at the Meeting with Asia Society (with Q&A)," September 24, 2022.

Reuters, "China Complains After Japanese Minister Visits Taiwan," *Newsweek*, March 27, 2017.

Robson, Seth, "US-Filipino Troops Kick Off New Kamandag Exercise in the Philippines," *Stars and Stripes*, October 2, 2017.

Romero, Paolo, "Tulfo Seeks Contingency Plan for OFWs in Taiwan," *Philippine Star*, August 8, 2022.

"S. Korea Has Refrained from Comments on China's Internal Affairs: FM," Yonhap News Agency, May 25, 2021. As of February 3, 2023: https://en.yna.co.kr/view/AEN20210525005500325

Sang-Hun, Choe, "In a First, South Korea Declares Nuclear Weapons a Policy Option," *New York Times*, January 12, 2023.

Schelling, Thomas C., *Arms and Influence*, Yale University Press, 1966.

Schmitt, Gary J., and Michael Mazza, "The End of 'Strategic Ambiguity' Regarding Taiwan," *The Dispatch*, September 17, 2020.

Serapio, Manolo, Jr., and Petty Martin, "Philippines' Duterte Says Pointless Discussing South China Sea Woes at Summit," Reuters, April 27, 2017.

Seung-woo, Kang, "Seoul Reiterates That '3 Nos' Policy Is Not Commitment to China," *Korea Times*, August 10, 2022.

Shenon, Philip, "Philippine Senate Votes to Reject U.S. Base Renewal," *New York Times*, September 16, 1991.

Shin, Hyonhee, "South Korea, China Clash over U.S. Missile Shield, Complicating Conciliation," Reuters, August 11, 2022a.

Shin, Hyonhee, "South Korea Urges Bigger China Role in Curbing North Korean Arms Tests," Reuters, November 15, 2022b.

Shirane, Seiji, "Imperial Gateway: Colonial Taiwan and Japan's Expansion in South China and Southeast Asia, 1895–1945," *Asia-Pacific Journal*, Vol. 20, No. 17, 2022.

"Should the United States Pledge to Defend Taiwan? Foreign Affairs Asks the Experts," *Foreign Affairs*, November 15, 2022.

Snyder, Glenn H., *Alliance Politics*, Cornell University Press, 1997.

Soeya, Yoshihide, "Taiwan in Japan's Security Considerations," *China Quarterly*, No. 165, March 1, 2001.

"Special Issue: 50 Years of Japan-China: Prospects for the Future" ["論点スペシャル] 日中５０年　将来を展望"], *Yomiuri Shimbun*, September 29, 2022.

Stiles, Matt, "Upset over a U.S. Missile Defense System, China Hits South Korea Where It Hurts—in the Wallet," *Los Angeles Times*, February 28, 2018.

Stolper, Thomas E., "China, Taiwan, and the Offshore Islands Together with an Implication for Outer Mongolia and Sino-Soviet Relations," *International Journal of Politics*, Vol. 15, No. 1/2, 1985.

Strangio, Sebastian, "Philippines' Marcos Pledges to Uphold Landmark South China Sea Ruling," *The Diplomat*, May 27, 2022a.

Strangio, Sebastian, "Philippines' Marcos to Pursue Bilateral Deal with Beijing over South China Sea," *The Diplomat*, January 28, 2022b.

Swaine, Michael D., "Taiwan's Management of Relations with the United States During the First Chen Shui-bian Administration," Carnegie Endowment for International Peace, May 5, 2005.

Tomacruz, Sofia, "In Turnaround, Marcos Pledges to Uphold Hague Ruling," Rappler.com, May 26, 2022. As of February 23, 2023: https://www.rappler.com/nation/ marcos-jr-pledges-uphold-hague-ruling-west-philippine-sea/

Treaty of Peace with Japan, September 8, 1951. As of February 22, 2023: https://treaties.un.org/doc/publication/unts/volume%20136/volume-136-i-1832-english.pdf

Twomey, Christopher P., "The Fourth Taiwan Strait Crisis Is Just Starting," *War on the Rocks*, August 22, 2022.

U.S. Department of Defense, *National Defense Strategy of the United States of America*, 2022.

U.S. Department of Defense, "Philippines, U.S. Announce Four New EDCA Sites," *DOD News*, February 1, 2023. As of February 9, 2023: https://www.defense.gov/News/Releases/Release/Article/3285566/philippines-us-announce-four-new-edca-sites/

U.S. Department of State, "Remarks: Secretary Antony J. Blinken and Philippine Secretary of Foreign Affairs Enrique Manalo at a Virtual Press Availability," August 6, 2022. As of February 3, 2023: https://www.state.gov/secretary-antony-j-blinken-and-philippine-secretary-of-foreign-affairs-enrique-manalo-at-a-virtual-press-availability/

U.S. Embassy and Consulates in Japan, "Joint Statement of the Security Consultative Committee (2+2)," January 11, 2023. As of February 22, 2023: https://jp.usembassy.gov/joint-statement-security-consultative-committee-2plus2/

U.S. Embassy in the Philippines, "37th Iteration of Balikatan Exercise Set to Begin in the Philippines," March 22, 2022. As of February 3, 2023: https://ph.usembassy.gov/37th-iteration-of-balikatan-exercise-set-to-begin-in-the-philippines/

U.S. House of Representatives, A Concurrent Resolution Expressing the Sense of Congress Regarding Missile Tests and Military Exercises by the People's Republic of China, Bill 148, March 21, 1996.

U.S. House of Representatives, "Reaffirming the Taiwan Relations Act and the Six Assurances as Cornerstones of United States–Taiwan Relations," H.Con. Res.88, 2016.

"U.S.-Japan Joint Leaders' Statement: U.S.-Japan Global Partnership for a New Era," April 16, 2021. As of December 1, 2022: https://www.whitehouse.gov/briefing-room/statements-releases/2021/04/16/u-s-japan-joint-leaders-statement-u-s-japan-global-partnership-for-a-new-era/

"U.S.-ROK Leaders' Joint Statement," May 21, 2021. As of February 3, 2023: https://www.whitehouse.gov/briefing-room/statements-releases/2021/05/21/u-s-rok-leaders-joint-statement/

"United States–Republic of Korea Leaders' Joint Statement," May 21, 2022. As of February 3, 2023: https://www.whitehouse.gov/briefing-room/statements-releases/2022/05/21/united-states-republic-of-korea-leaders-joint-statement/

"US, Philippines Launch War Games Amid Uncertainty over Ties," *DW*, October 4, 2016.

"US, Philippines to Restart Joint Patrols in South China Sea," *Defense Post*, February 3, 2023. As of February 22, 2023:
https://www.thedefensepost.com/2023/02/03/
us-philippines-patrols-south-china-sea/

Van Staaveren, Jacob, *Air Operations in the Taiwan Crisis of 1958*, USAF Historical Division Liaison Office, 1962.

"The Virtues of a Confrontational China Strategy," *American Interest*, April 10, 2020.

Weisiger, Alex, *Logics of War: Explanations for Limited and Unlimited Conflicts*, Cornell University Press, 2013.

Wertheim, Stephen, "On Taiwan, President Biden Should Listen to Senator Biden," Carnegie Endowment for International Peace, commentary, September 20, 2022.

The White House, *National Security Strategy*, October 1, 2022.

The White House, "Remarks by President Biden in a CNN Town Hall with Anderson Cooper," October 21, 2021. As of February 2, 2023:
https://www.whitehouse.gov/briefing-room/speeches-remarks/2021/10/22/
remarks-by-president-biden-in-a-cnn-town-hall-with-anderson-cooper-2/

"White House Backtracks After Biden Appears to Say US Would Defend Taiwan Against China," *The Guardian*, August 19, 2021.

Whiting, Allen S., "New Light on Mao: 3. Quemoy 1958: Mao's Miscalculations," *China Quarterly*, Vol. 62, 1975.

Whyte, Leon, "Evolution of the U.S.-ROK Alliance: Abandonment Fears," *The Diplomat*, June 22, 2015.

Yamaguchi, Mari, "Japan, Philippines Agree to Sharply Boost Defense Ties," AP News, February 9, 2023.

Yeo, Andrew, *Activists, Alliances, and Anti-U.S. Base Protests*, Cambridge University Press, 2011.

Yoshida, Shigeru, "Japan and the Crisis in Asia," *Foreign Affairs*, No. 29, 1951.